"Professor Maxwell Johnson of the University of Notre Dame has written a short but fulsome account of the influence of the liturgy on the development of the doctrines of grace, Trinity, Christology, and Mariology in the ancient Church and on early Christianity's moral practices. Entering into current debates in liturgical theology, Johnson challenges claims about liturgy and prayer as primary theology (*lex orandi*) and disagrees with the understanding of *orthodoxia* as 'right praise' (it is 'right teaching'). Rather, he sees a simultaneous development of both liturgy and dogma in the early centuries in which one should look for the theology embedded in the liturgy and doxology and supplication expressed in theology. While Johnson aimed this book at master's level students, it will be of interest also to his peers, who will find points to challenge precisely because they are so engagingly made."

—The Rev. Dr. Frank C. Senn, STS

"Finally! A renowned historian of liturgy explores at length the creative interplay between liturgical practice and theological reflection. This has been a desideratum for some time now, especially given the fresh readings of early Christian sources and the glimpses these provide of liturgical practices. In his new book, Max Johnson offers a nuanced, carefully argued, and expertly corroborated look at how doctrine shaped liturgical prayer and how prayer shaped the church's faith in the early centuries. Mapping the interplay between praying and believing in a multidimensional way, Johnson makes an important and much needed contribution to the ongoing conversation about the relationship between worship and doctrine in the church's life. I highly recommend this book."

—Teresa Berger
Yale Institute of Sacred Music
Yale Divinity School

Maxwell E. Johnson

Praying and Believing in Early Christianity

The Interplay between Christian Worship and Doctrine

A Michael Glazier Book

LITURGICAL PRESS
Collegeville, Minnesota

www.litpress.org

A Michael Glazier Book published by Liturgical Press

Cover design by Jodi Hendrickson. Cover image: Eucharist—Sacrificial Banquet Icon by Monsignor Anthony A. La Femina, STL, JCD. Used by permission.

1	2	3	4	5	6	7	8	9

Library of Congress Cataloging-in-Publication Data

Johnson, Maxwell E., 1952–
    Praying and believing in early Christianity : the interplay between Christian worship and doctrine / Maxwell E. Johnson.
        pages   cm
    "A Michael Glazier book."
    Includes index.
    ISBN 978-0-8146-8259-3 (pbk. : alk. paper) — ISBN 978-0-8146-8284-5 (e-book)
    1. Worship—History—Early church, ca. 30–600.   2. Church history—Primitive and early church, ca. 30–600.   I. Title.
BV6.J645   2013
270.1—dc23   2013007002

In Memoriam
R. Kevin Seasoltz, OSB (+ 2013)
Teacher, Colleague, and Friend

Contents

Abbreviations

ANF   Ante-Nicene Fathers

BCE   Before the Common Era

CE   Common Era

CSEL   Corpus Scriptorum Ecclesiasticorum Latinorum

GCS   Die griechischen christlichen Schriftsteller

LCC   Library of Christian Classics

LEW   F. E. Brightman, *Liturgies Eastern and Western*, vol. 1:
        Eastern Liturgies. Oxford: Clarendon Press, 1896.

NPNF   Nicene and Post-Nicene Fathers

PEER   *Prayers of the Eucharist: Early and Reformed*, edited by
        R. C. D. Jasper and G. J. Cumming. 3rd rev. ed.
        Collegeville, MN: Liturgical Press, 1987.

PG   Patrologia Graeca

PL   Patrologia Latina

SC   Sources chrétiennes

Introduction

I remember hearing part of a conversation between two of my seminary professors—one, a professor of New Testament at the Lutheran seminary where I was enrolled, and the other, a professor of liturgy at the neighboring Roman Catholic seminary, where in the spring semester of 1975 I was taking my first serious course in liturgical history—over the proper place of liturgy in the seminary curriculum. For the Lutheran professor, the place of liturgy was to be included naturally in the "Practical Area" of seminary education along with parish administration, homiletics, parish education, and pastoral care and counseling, since, in his opinion, the study of liturgy had more to do with the practicalities of presiding at worship than with theology and/or history. For the Roman Catholic faculty member, however, liturgy naturally was to be included in the "History and Theology Area" of the curriculum both because liturgy constituted an academic discipline in its own right and because he saw liturgy having a historic and foundational relationship to theology and doctrine in general. To my knowledge, this discussion never reached a resolution with courses in liturgy at the Lutheran seminary remaining in the "Practical Area" and those at the Roman Catholic seminary in the "History and Theology Area," although courses in presiding at the rites themselves were taught there within the practical area as well.

This discussion has implications for the question of *liturgical* theology today along the lines of the classic relationship between liturgy and doctrine, often summarized by the abbreviated Latin phrase of Prosper of Aquitaine (c. 390–c. 455): *"Lex orandi, lex credendi,"* i.e., the "law of praying (is, constitutes, or establishes) the law of believing." For the Lutheran faculty member referred to above, although these words would not have been used, the *lex credendi* (especially Lutheran confessional and sacramental theology) was to be learned independently of the church's liturgy and then, perhaps, applied to what one *did* in liturgy. Hence, to put words in this professor's mouth, the relationship was that the *lex credendi* always established the *lex orandi* and, of course, the *lex credendi* was always, therefore, primary.

For the Roman Catholic professor, it was the exact opposite, with the *lex orandi* itself establishing or constituting the church's *lex credendi* in the first place, a position argued strongly in recent years by Aidan Kavanagh in his insistence on the need for the use of the verb *statuo* in Prosper's actual phrase, i.e., *ut legem credendi lex statuat supplicandi,* "that the law of supplicating *may constitute* the law of believing."[1] If, for the Lutheran professor, liturgy was rather superfluous to the overall theological process and, hence, could be easily relegated out of the realm of "real" theology, for the Roman Catholic professor, liturgy was quite central in and for all areas of seminary formation and pastoral-ecclesial life. It was thus too important to be so easily separated from theology and history and subsumed under practical matters alone.

I have always tended to side with this Roman Catholic faculty member regarding the formative role of liturgy, the role of the *lex orandi* in the church's theological and doctrinal self-expression, and where the study of liturgy belongs in the academic curriculum. To borrow from the title of the now classic 1985 book by Leonel L. Mitchell, I firmly hold that "praying shapes believing."[2] That is, while not the only criterion for doing so, one can—or *should* be able to—read the theology, belief, and doctrines of any given church by means of what its liturgies pray, say, sing, and direct.

If such a liturgical text or liturgical content-based approach was once commonly accepted in the subdiscipline of liturgical studies called liturgical theology, however, today that subdiscipline can be divided into at least two different schools of thought or methodological approaches. These have been well summarized in a 2007 two-part *Worship* article by Michael Aune titled "Liturgy and Theology: Rethinking the Relationship."[3] The first school of thought Aune calls the "Schmemann-Kavanagh-Fagerberg-Lathrop line of liturgical the-

---

[1] Aidan Kavanagh, *On Liturgical Theology* (New York: Pueblo, 1984). I have critiqued Kavanagh's position elsewhere. See my essay, "Liturgy and Theology," in *Liturgy in Dialogue*, ed., Paul Bradshaw and Bryan Spinks (London: SPCK, 1993), 202–25.

[2] Leonel L. Mitchell, *Praying Shapes Believing: A Theological Commentary* on The Book of Common Prayer (Harrisburg, PA: Morehouse Publishing, 1985).

[3] Michael Aune, "Liturgy and Theology: Rethinking the Relationship, Part 1, Setting the Stage," *Worship* 81, no. 1 (January 2007): 46–68; "Liturgy and Theology:

ology," after the important and influential writings on the topic by
Alexander Schmemann,[4] Aidan Kavanagh,[5] David Fagerberg,[6] and
Gordon Lathrop.[7] According to Aune, what these scholars have in
common is a shared methodology that tends to take ecclesiology,
the liturgical assembly, and/or the actual experience of Christian
worship by communities and individuals as its starting point. In
other words, liturgical theology is based on what is *done* by the liturgical assembly as the primary active agent in liturgy and what the
assembly encounters and experiences in that event. One might call
this approach a liturgical theology from the "bottom up." According
to Aune, this approach is often related to a common (mis-)under-
standing of the word "liturgy" itself, *leitourgia*, as meaning "work
of the people," comprised by two Greek words: *laos* (people) and
ergon (work). As Paul Marshall demonstrated over fifteen years ago,
however, that interpretation is simply incorrect.[8] Rather, as Marshall
notes correctly, the etymology of *leitourgia* is *ergon* (work) and *leitos*
(public). It is a secular Greek term for a *public* work done not by but
on *behalf* of the people by another person or group appointed to that
task, a term equivalent to those public officials in countries such
as England designated as "ministers" (e.g., the prime minister). In

Rethinking the Relationship, Part 2, A Different Starting Place," *Worship* 81, no.
2 (March 2007): 141–69.

[4] Alexander Schmemann, *Introduction to Liturgical Theology*, 2nd ed. (Crestwood,
NY: St. Vladimir's Seminary Press, 1975); *For the Life of the World* (Crestwood, NY:
St. Vladimir's Seminary Press, 1973); "Liturgical Theology, Theology of Liturgy,
and Liturgical Reform," *St. Vladimir's Theological Quarterly* (1969): 217–24; and
"Liturgy and Theology," *The Greek Orthodox Theological Review* 17 (1972): 86–100.
Thomas Fisch has edited a collection of Schmemann's essays on this topic in *Lit-
urgy and Tradition: Theological Reflections of Alexander Schmemann* (Crestwood, NY:
St. Vladimir's Seminary Press, 1990).

[5] Kavanagh, *On Liturgical Theology*.

[6] David Fagerberg, *What Is Liturgical Theology? A Study in Methodology* (College-
ville, MN: Liturgical Press, 1992). See his second revised edition, *Theologia Prima:
What Is Liturgical Theology* (Chicago: Liturgical Training Publications, Hillenbrand
Books, 2004).

[7] Gordon Lathrop, *Holy Things: A Liturgical Theology* (Minneapolis: Fortress Press,
1993).

[8] Paul Marshall, "Reconsidering 'Liturgical Theology': Is There a *Lex Orandi*
for All Christians?," *Studia Liturgica* 25 (1995): 129–51.

fact, in the New Testament the primary use of this term is for Christ himself, whom the Letter to the Hebrews (8:2) designates precisely as our *leitourgos*!

As representative of the second school of thought, Aune himself juxtaposes a more "top down" approach, arguing that what is needed in liturgical theology is less focus on the community, assembly, or even liturgy as communal "action," and a better theological concentration on what *God* does in liturgy, "especially focusing on God's self-communication in this event and, as a result, reemphasizing the divine agency and initiative."[9] In addition to this, Aune calls for a more up-to-date grasp of historical liturgical scholarship among liturgical theologians today. Here he echoes Paul Bradshaw's critique that much contemporary liturgical theology "rests upon bad history or no history at all,"[10] often treating a selective reading of especially patristic liturgical sources and reconstructed rites as constituting a sort of normative or golden age of liturgy with both medieval and Reformation developments seen automatically as aberrations. Aune draws particular attention to liturgical historians such as Bradshaw,[11] Gabriele Winkler,[12] Robert Taft,[13] and me[14] in his call to take liturgical historical scholarship with more seriousness in the theological endeavor. And he points us to alternative contemporary liturgical theologians like

[9] Aune, "Liturgy and Theology, Part 2," 142.

[10] Paul Bradshaw, "Difficulties in Doing Liturgical Theology," *Pacifica* 11 (June 1998): 193.

[11] Paul Bradshaw, *The Search for the Origins of Christian Worship*, 2nd rev. ed. (London: SPCK, 2002).

[12] Aune refers especially to Winkler's work on the *Sanctus*. See Gabriele Winkler, *Das Sanctus. Über den Ursprung und die Anfänge des Sanctus und sein Fortwirken*, Orientalia Christiana Analecta 267 (Rome: Pontificio Istituto Orientale, 2002).

[13] Robert Taft, "What Does Liturgy Do? Toward a Soteriology of Liturgical Celebration: Some Theses," in *Beyond East and West: Problems in Liturgical Understanding*, 2nd rev. and enlarged ed. (Rome: Pontifical Oriental Institute, 1997).

[14] Maxwell E. Johnson, "Can We Avoid Relativism in Worship? Liturgical Norms in the Light of Contemporary Liturgical Scholarship," *Worship* 74, no. 2 (March 2000): 135–54.

Kevin Irwin,[15] Reinhard Meßner,[16] Reinhold Malcherek,[17] Edward
Kilmartin,[18] and Pope Benedict XVI[19] for support for this emphasis
on recovering God's activity in the liturgy and for what might be
called a "Christocentric" or "Theocentric" rather than "ecclesiocen-
tric" approach.

As one who is primarily a liturgical historian in terms of methodology, it is not my intent in this study to take one side or the other in this
contemporary debate, especially because I have strong sympathies
toward both approaches. Indeed, it would be difficult for me to dis-
agree with Aune's concerns for taking historical-liturgical scholarship
more seriously or for underscoring theologically the divine initiative
in worship, that liturgy, in the words of Nathan Mitchell, following
the Rule of St. Benedict, is *"opus Dei,"* something "beautiful that God
does for us."[20] But, at the same time, the other approach remains
most helpful even in articulating God's self-communication in the
liturgical event, for orthodox Christian faith is at the same time the
faith of the *church* that is expressed, celebrated, renewed, and, hence,
continually constituted in the liturgical assembly as it enacts those
very "holy things" (Lathrop) that the Church *does* in obedience to the
biblical command of Christ: "Do this . . ."

My focus in this book, however, is much more modest than trying
to resolve the contemporary debates as to what constitutes liturgical
theology. Others can and should do that. Rather, written primarily

[15] Kevin Irwin, "A Spirited Community Encounters Christ: Liturgical and
Sacramental Theology and Practice," in *Catholic Theology Facing the Future: Historical Perspectives*, ed. Dermot A. Lane (Mahwah, NJ: Paulist Press, 2003), 95–124.

[16] Reinhard Meßner, *Einführung in die Liturgiewissenschaft* (Paderborn: Ferdinand
Schöningh, 2001). See also idem, "Was ist systematische Liturgiewissenschaft?
Ein Entwurf in sieben Thesen," *Archiv für Liturgiewissenschaft* 40 (1988): 257–74.

[17] Reinhold Malcherek, "Gemeinshaft von Gott und den Menschen: Überle-
gungen zur Liturgie als gottmenschlicher Dialog nach der Liturgiekonstitution
des II. Vatikanischen Konzils," *Ecclesia Orans* 18 (2001): 237–68.

[18] Edward Kilmartin, *Christian Liturgy: Theology and Practice*, vol. 1: *Systematic
Theology* (Kansas City: Sheed & Ward, 1988).

[19] Benedict XVI (Cardinal Joseph Ratzinger), *A New Song for the Lord: Faith in
Christ and Liturgy Today* (New York: Crossroad, 1996), and idem, *The Spirit of the
Liturgy* (San Francisco: Ignatius Press, 2000).

[20] Nathan Mitchell, "The Amen Corner: Being Good and Being Beautiful,"
Worship 74, no. 6 (November 2000): 557–58.

for beginning students in liturgical studies at the master's level, this book is about the relationship of liturgy in early Christianity to the development of orthodox Christian belief in terms of soteriology, trinitarian theology, Christology, Mariology, and ethics. How, in each of these cases, did worship assist in the shaping of what was believed, taught, and confessed? And, of course, in addition to relevant extant descriptions of worship, that also means attention to texts where they are available, for the textual content of that worship is theologically and doctrinally significant. If there is any contemporary liturgical theologian I find myself most in sympathy with in this endeavor, it is clearly the British Methodist Geoffrey Wainwright,[21] to whom my indebtedness will be demonstrated time and again in the following pages of this work.

At the same time, it needs to be noted that this book is not a study of the development of doctrine itself. In fact, while occasional details of doctrinal development are provided and definitions of certain terms are offered, I assume that the reader already has some knowledge and, at least, broad understanding of the chief figures, doctrinal controversies, and their resolutions at the first four ecumenical councils (Nicea in 325 CE, Constantinople in 381 CE, Ephesus in 431 CE, and Chalcedon in 451 CE) as well as the controversies between Augustine (and others) with Pelagianism and "Semi-Pelagianism" over the question of grace and nature. In any event, such studies are readily available for those who seek additional detailed information.[22]

---

[21] Geoffrey Wainwright, *Doxology: The Praise of God in Worship, Doctrine, and Life* (New York: Oxford University Press, 1980).

[22] See, in particular, Jaroslav Pelikan, *The Christian Tradition: A History of the Development of Doctrine*, vol.1: *The Emergence of the Catholic Tradition (100–600)* (Chicago: University of Chicago Press, 1971); idem, *Credo: Historical and Theological Guide to Creeds and Confessions of Faith in the Christian Tradition* (New Haven, CT: Yale University Press, 2003); and, with specific regard to the councils of Ephesus and Chalcedon, the recent work by Philip Jenkins, *The Jesus Wars: How Four Patriarchs, Three Queens, and Two Emperors Decided What Christians Would Believe for the Next 1,500 Years* (New York: HarperOne, 2010). With specific regard to the Arian Controversy, see Rowan Williams, *Arius: Heresy and Tradition*, rev. and exp. ed. (Grand Rapids, MI: Eerdmans, 2001). For relevant primary texts in translation see William G. Rusch, ed., *The Trinitarian Controversy* (Philadelphia:

This book is organized in the following manner. Chapter 1, "Liturgical Praying and the Priority of Grace," deals with soteriology, the role of grace in the process of salvation. In fact, as will be seen, the question of the role of grace in the controversies over Pelagianism and Semi-Pelagianism is precisely the issue that gives rise to the famous axiom of Prosper, "*ut legem credendi lex statuat supplicandi,*" in the first place. As part of this chapter it will also be important to distinguish what this phrase means and does *not* mean, as well as provide an evaluative critique of its authority in looking at liturgy as a *locus theologicus* in general. Chapter 2, "Doxology and Trinity," treats the relationship between early devotion to Christ and the liturgical prayer of the church, especially in its baptismal and eucharistic liturgies, to the developing doctrine of the Trinity at the councils of Nicea (325 CE) and Constantinople I (381 CE). While much of this will probably be familiar territory to many readers, it is this particular trinitarian topic, i.e., the relationship of Christ the Son to God the Father, and the relationship of the Holy Spirit to them both, where scholarship—liturgical and otherwise—has been the most sensitive to the role of worship in their formulations. Chapter 3, "Christ and Mary," is concerned with the further development of Christology after the councils of Nicea and Constantinople, especially with regard to the devotional and liturgical development and context of the term *Theotokos,* "God bearer," as the title *par excellence* for the Blessed Virgin Mary in relation to the identity and personhood of Christ adopted against the "Nestorian" position at the Council of Ephesus (431 CE). While the *christological* significance of this title is widely acknowledged and accepted, the mariological context and potential implications have often not been taken as seriously. A good portion of this chapter, then, is based on and provides an update of earlier work I have done on the subject,[23] although it goes beyond this to the liturgical context and implications of the Council of Chalcedon (451 CE) as well. Chapter 4, "Worship

---

Fortress Press, 1980); and Richard A. Norris Jr., ed., *The Christological Controversy* (Philadelphia: Fortress Press, 1980).

[23] See my "*Sub Tuum Praesidium*: The *Theotokos* in Christian Life and Worship before Ephesus," in *The Place of Christ in Liturgical Prayer: Christology, Trinity and Liturgical Theology,* ed. Bryan D. Spinks (Collegeville, MN: Liturgical Press, 2008), 243–67.

and Praxis," looks at the relationship between what is prayed in liturgy and how life is to be lived in the world as a result of that prayer. In other words, does the liturgy contribute to shaping not only doctrine but also ethics? Such an approach is often taken for granted in contemporary approaches to liturgy and justice or liturgy and ethics. But this asks the similar question with regard to early Christianity. Are there indications of that concern not so much in texts of the liturgy but in comments and homiletical reflections on the meaning of the liturgy for the life of Christians in antiquity? And, finally, since doctrine also shapes liturgy, especially its theological-textual content, the concluding chapter, chapter 5, "Conclusion: Praying and Believing Together," looks at how the doctrinal developments treated above come to give lasting shape to the liturgical texts of both East and West in the patristic period.

Since I am concerned principally in this study with the relationship of Christian worship to the development of *orthodox* Christian doctrine and faith, it is important here to clear up a widespread assumption and confusion about that relationship. One still too frequently hears that the word "orthodoxy" is related etymologically to the Greek words *doxa* ("glory") and *ortho* ("right" or "correct") and that "orthodoxy" therefore means literally "right glory," a position that the Russian word for "orthodoxy" (*Pravoslavie*), it must be said, does tend to support. Nevertheless, while it is certainly true that doxology does lead to and help shape orthodoxy, in patristic Greek the word "orthodoxy" itself is comprised not by *ortho* and *doxa* but by *ortho* and the verb *dokeo*, which means to teach or think, or, again as Paul Marshall has demonstrated, following the Greek verb *orthodoxologeo*, meaning "to hold the correct opinion."[24] "Orthodoxy," therefore, is about holding the correct *doctrinal teaching* and not about giving "right glory" to God liturgically.

Finally, I wish to acknowledge gratefully several people who made this study possible: to my Notre Dame colleague Professor Paul Bradshaw who read every chapter and offered his most helpful critique; to Professor Bernard Evans of the School of Theology, Saint John's University, Collegeville, Minnesota, and to Professor Alan Kreider of

---

[24] Marshall, "Reconsidering 'Liturgical Theology,'" 142. See also G. W. H. Lampe, *A Patristic Greek Lexicon* (Oxford: Clarendon Press, 1965), 971.

the Associated Mennonite Biblical Seminary in Elkhart, Indiana, for their critical reflections and comments on chapter 4; to my graduate assistant Katharine Mahon for her assistance in research, proofreading, and indexing; and, not least, to Hans Christoffersen and Liturgical Press for guiding this to publication under the Michael Glazier imprint. To all of these I am indeed most grateful.

Maxwell E. Johnson
June 29, 2013
Saints Peter and Paul, Apostles

Chapter 1

Liturgical Praying and the Priority of Grace

In his now classic *Doxology: The Praise of God in Worship, Doctrine, and Life*,[1] Geoffrey Wainwright compares the distinct and traditional approaches of Roman Catholicism and Protestantism to what he refers to as a "Latin tag in modern usage," namely, the principle of "*lex orandi, lex credendi*," noting that:

> Roman Catholicism characteristically appeals to existing liturgical practice for proof in matters of doctrine. There *lex orandi, lex credendi* is most readily taken to make the (descriptive) pattern of prayer a (prescriptive) norm for belief, so that what is prayed indicates what may and must be believed. Protestantism characteristically emphasizes the primacy of doctrine over the liturgy. The phrase *lex orandi, lex credendi* is not well known among Protestants, but they would most easily take the dogmatic norm of belief as setting a rule for prayer, so that what must be believed governs what may and should be prayed.[2]

While Wainwright's own work made a large contribution to overcoming this distinctive denominational or tradition-specific approach to the topic, one might surely question why for Protestants such resistance to liturgy as a *locus theologicus* was traditionally the case in the first place. For, as we shall see, the appeal that Prosper of Aquitaine, disciple of Augustine and Gallican monk at Louvain, makes to the liturgy is one made precisely in defense of the necessity of divine grace, on "reemphasizing the divine agency and initiative"[3] in salvation and

---

[1] Geoffrey Wainwright, *Doxology: The Praise of God in Worship, Doctrine, and Life; A Systematic Theology* (New York and London: Oxford University Press, 1980).

[2] Ibid., 251.

[3] Michael Aune, "Liturgy and Theology: Rethinking the Relationship, Part 2, A Different Starting Place," *Worship* 81, no. 2 (March 2007): 142.

every act, a role that would seem quite consistent with a Protestant theological stance and method.

It is, in fact, within the context of the fifth-century semi-Pelagian controversy, and in his defense of the need for divine grace in salvation, that Prosper of Aquitaine refers to the church's liturgical supplication for grace and, in so doing, expresses what has become the influential principle for much of contemporary liturgical theology: *ut legem credendi lex statuat supplicandi.*

> In inviolable decrees of the blessed apostolic see, our holy fathers have cast down the pride of this pestiferous novelty and taught us to ascribe to the grace of Christ the very beginnings of good will, the growth of noble efforts, and the perseverance in them to the end. In addition, let us look at the sacred testimony of priestly intercessions which have been transmitted from the apostles and which are uniformly celebrated throughout the world and in every catholic church; so that the law of prayer may establish a law for belief [*ut legem credendi lex statuat supplicandi*]. For when the presidents of the holy congregations perform their duties, they plead the cause of the human race before the divine clemency and, joined by the sighs of the whole church, they beg and pray that grace may be given to unbelievers; that idolaters may be freed from the errors of their impiety; that the Jews may have the veil removed from their hearts and that the light of truth may shine on them; that heretics may recover through acceptance of the catholic faith; that schismatics may receive afresh the spirit of charity; that the lapsed may be granted the remedy of penitence; and finally that the catechumens may be brought to the sacrament of regeneration and have the court of the heavenly mercy opened to them.[4]

In order to understand the particular semi-Pelagian context of Prosper's statement, however, it is first necessary to discuss Pelagianism and semi-Pelagianism themselves and the response of Augustine.

1. Liturgy and the Pelagian and Semi-Pelagian Controversies

Whatever the precise relationship between the British monk Pelagius himself (ca. 400) and "Pelagianism" might actually have been,

---

[4] *Capitula Coelestini 8* (Migne, *Patrologia Latina* 51:205–12), As translated by Wainwright, *Doxology*, 225–26.

this theological position maintained that human beings, like Adam in the Garden of Eden before the Fall, are born with absolute free will and are able to choose and turn to good as well as evil. In other words, human beings have been created with the possibility of obeying the law of God perfectly and by so doing come to merit an eternal reward from God. While Adam's sin did bring about the consequences of suffering and death for humanity, the human will itself was unaffected and remained essentially free.[5]

It was primarily in response to the challenges against the widespread practice and long tradition of infant baptism in North Africa by Celestius, a disciple of Pelagius, who came to North Africa from Rome after the sack of Rome in 410, that Augustine develops what has come to be called the theology of "original sin." Contrary to the Pelagian position, Augustine argued that the human will is not free but sick, "curved in upon itself" (*incurvatus in se ipsum*), and seeks only the gratification of its own self-oriented desires (a condition of "concupiscence" or "lust"). Hence, from the moment of their birth, human beings *cannot* choose, will, or do what is good but are in need of the medicine of divine grace in order to choose, will, and do the good. It is this prevenient grace that is necessary in order to heal the will and orient it away from the sinful self to God, who will then continue to grant grace for every good desire and act. Human nature, then, is mortally wounded by sin. And if this sin is not cured by the divine Physician's medicine of grace, it becomes the source of all other sin. Without this cure of divine grace, humanity remains a *massa damnata*, a "condemned mass," and those who die unbaptized are not saved, a position that was unacceptable to the later Western church.

The cause of this human sickness leading to condemnation, for Augustine, of course, is the sin of Adam himself, which has been transmitted to all human beings along with suffering and death. Although he refuses to commit himself to any one philosophical position on the precise "moment" when this original sin is transmitted to any particular human being, it is clear that for him it is connected

---

[5] On Pelagianism in general, see Jaroslav Pelikan, *The Christian Tradition: A History of the Development of Doctrine*, vol.1: *The Emergence of the Catholic Tradition (100–600)* (Chicago: University of Chicago Press, 1971), 278–331; and W. H. C. Frend, *The Rise of Christianity* (Philadephia: Fortress Press, 1984), 673–83.

somehow to the process of human reproduction, especially as the sexual act itself is related to sexual "desire." That is, "Augustine clearly taught that original sin and guilt are derived from the act of procreation, 'in virtue of the lustful promptings of his body . . . to serve the purpose of propagation.'"[6]

Augustine's theology was based in part on the fact that rites of exorcism in baptism demonstrated the obvious need for *all* candidates—both adults and infants—to be liberated from sin, death, and the devil.[7] If baptism is for the forgiveness of sin, then the fact that infants are baptized (a practice which antedates any theological rationale for it!) obviously indicates that they are in need of forgiveness. Here, before Prosper, then, is a *lex orandi, lex credendi* argument based not only on texts but on actual liturgical practice as well.

Since for Augustine the rite and practice of infant baptism play a special role in this controversy, appeal is often made to his theology to support the necessity of infant baptism in the life of the church.[8] One must never assume, however, that infant initiation became some kind of normative practice in his time or even immediately thereafter. In fact, as Mark Searle has shown, while Augustine himself had developed his theology of original sin based, in part, on the already existing practice of infant baptism within the North African church of the fourth and fifth centuries, it was really only later, well after the time of Augustine, that infant baptism itself became regularly mandated in the West:

> In the ninth century Walafrid Strabo reversed Augustine's argument: "Since all who are not delivered by God's grace will perish in original sin, including those who have not added to it by their own personal sin, it is necessary to baptize infants." Thereafter the practice of infant

---

[6] Carl Volz, *Faith and Practice in the Early Church: Foundations for Contemporary Theology* (Minneapolis: Augsburg Publishing House, 1983), 55.

[7] On the rite of baptism known by Augustine, see Maxwell E. Johnson, *The Rites of Christian Initiation: Their Evolution and Interpretation*, 2nd rev. ed. (Collegeville, MN: Liturgical Press, Pueblo, 2007), 185ff.; and William Harmless, *Augustine and the Catechumenate* (Collegeville, MN: Liturgical Press, Pueblo, 1995).

[8] On Augustine and infant baptism in general, see R. de Latte, "Saint Augustin et le baptême. Étude liturgico-historique du rituel baptismal des enfants chez saint Augustin," *Questions Liturgiques* 57, no. 1 (1976): 41–55.

baptism will be justified on the basis of the doctrine of original sin, not vice versa.[9]

Furthermore, Anthony N. S. Lane[10] has shown recently that through the fourth century the churches were able to tolerate a rather wide diversity of practice with regard to infant initiation, with the biggest motivation *against* it—even for the children of Christian parents—being the fear of postbaptismal sin and its consequences. While some parents certainly had their children initiated as infants, others did not, and it appears that both practices were seen as legitimate. Even someone in the Christian East like Gregory of Nazianzus could advocate both the almost immediate "sanctification" of children, especially those in danger of death, as well as delaying their initiation until the age of three. Pope Siricius in 385 urged infant baptism out of a fear of them dying unbaptized, but, at roughly the same time, Monica had only enrolled Augustine in the catechumenate as an infant and had not had him initiated.[11]

Liturgically, however, more is at stake here for Augustine than the presence of exorcisms in baptism or the actual rite of baptism functioning as a theological or doctrinal source. Rather, as Paul De Clerck demonstrated in a 1978 French article[12] (which appeared in English

---

[9] Mark Searle, "Infant Baptism Reconsidered," in *Living Water, Sealing Spirit: Readings on Christian Initiation*, ed. Maxwell E. Johnson (Collegeville, MN: Liturgical Press, Pueblo, 1995), 375.

[10] Anthony N. S. Lane, "Did the Apostolic Church Baptise Babies? A Seismological Approach," *Tyndale Bulletin* 55, no. 1 (2004): 121–23. Lane's work takes note of several significant studies by David F. Wright, "How Controversial Was the Development of Infant Baptism in the Early Church?," in *Church, Word, and Spirit*, ed. J. E. Bradley and R. A. Muller (Grand Rapids, MI: Eerdmans, 1987), 45–63; "At What Age Were People Baptized in the Early Centuries?," *Studia Patristica* 30 (1997): 389–94; and "Infant Dedication in the Early Church," in *Baptism, the New Testament and the Church: Historical and Contemporary Studies in Honour of R.E.O. White*, ed. Stanley E. Porter and Anthony R. Cross, Journal for the Study of the New Testament Supplement Series 171 (Sheffield; Sheffield Academic Press, 1999), 352–78.

[11] See David F. Wright, "Monica's Baptism, Augustine's Deferred Baptism, and Patricius," *Augustinian Studies* 29 (1998): 1–17.

[12] Paul De Clerck, "'Lex orandi, lex credendi': Sens originel et avatars historiques d'un adage équivoque," *Questions Liturgiques* 59 (1978): 193–212.

only sixteen years later[13]), Augustine "constantly made appeal" to liturgical texts and practice in his response to Pelagianism and later to semi-Pelagianism. In fact, Augustine's own formula, which never quite captured the imagination of liturgical theologians in the same way as Prosper's, is *"ipsa igitur oratio clarissima est gratiae testificatio"* ("prayer itself, therefore, is the clearest testimony of grace").[14] Further, in a letter (ca. 427) to a semi-Pelagian leader in the church at Carthage named Vitalis, Augustine again argues on the basis of the prayer of the church:

> Therefore, affirm openly that we ought not to pray that those to whom we preach the Gospel may believe, but that it suffices to preach to them. Give your criticisms against the prayers of the Church, and when you hear the priest of God at the altar exhorting the people of God to pray for unbelievers that God might convert them to the faith, and for the catechumens that he might inspire them to desire regeneration, and for the faithful that by his grace they might persevere in that which they have begun to be, then make fun of these pious words, and affirm clearly that you do not do what the priest exhorts you to do, that is to say, that you do not pray to God for the unbelievers that he might make believers out of them. (Dare to say this clearly) because you do believe that this conversion is not the work of divine mercy, but the labor of the human will. And you, an educated man in the church of Carthage, condemn also then the commentary of St Cyprian on the Lord's Prayer; for this doctor shows that it is necessary to ask of God our Father that which you, on your part, affirm that man ought to request of man, that is to say, of himself.[15]

The above citation not only demonstrates clearly Augustine's own use of liturgical prayer as a theological-doctrinal source in this controversy but also, like Prosper's own formulation of the *"lex supplicandi"* argument, gives us a window into so-called semi-Pelagianism itself. For, after the condemnation of Pelagianism, first in North Africa at

---

[13] Paul De Clerck, "'Lex orandi, lex credendi': The Original Sense and Historical Avatars of an Equivocal Age," *Studia Liturgica* 24 (1994): 178–200. All references in this study to the work of De Clerck are to the English translation.

[14] Latin text as cited in ibid., from Augustine, *Ep.* 177.4 (CSEL 44:673). The English translation is my own.

[15] Text as cited in De Clerk, "'Lex orandi, lex credendi': The Original Sense," 189–90. For the Latin text, see Augustine, *Ep.* 217.2 (CSEL 57:404).

a Synod of Carthage in 418 and then at the Ecumenical Council of Ephesus in 431, a somewhat modified version of this position developed, which, since the Protestant Reformers in the sixteenth century in a very different context, has been designated by the more recent term "semi-Pelagian."[16]

Semi-Pelagianism, often associated with the writings of John Cassian, St. Vincent of Lérins, and Faustus of Riez, may be characterized as a *via media* between the theological approaches of Augustine and Pelagius. At least, as popularly understood, and as understood by its critics at the time, if fundamental agreement was reached on the necessity of divine grace for human salvation, those ascribing to a semi-Pelagianist position taught that the first steps to salvation were still up to the free human will, which was then aided eventually by grace, i.e., "divine assistance," to complete the saving process. Such "semi-Pelagians" did not deny the Augustinian doctrines of original sin and grace and certainly did not teach a theology of salvation by human works rather than grace. And while the real issue, in fact, was the strict predestinarian position of Augustine (some are predestined to salvation, others to damnation), which they dismissed as a kind of Manichean fatalism, critics of the semi-Pelagians, like St. Fulgentius of Ruspe, St. Caesarius of Arles, and Prosper of Aquitaine himself, centered on the necessity of divine grace and initiative at the beginning, middle, and end of the order of salvation. It was all by grace and dependent on grace. Recall what Augustine writes to Vitalis:

> Give your criticisms against the prayers of the Church . . . when you hear the priest of God at the altar exhorting the people of God to pray for unbelievers that God might convert them to the faith, and for the catechumens that he might inspire them to desire regeneration, and for the faithful that by his grace they might persevere.

And, quite similarly, Prosper begins his treatment of the issue:

> In inviolable decrees of the blessed apostolic see, our holy fathers have cast down the pride of this pestiferous novelty and taught us to ascribe to the grace of Christ the very beginnings of good will, the growth of noble efforts, and the perseverance in them to the end.

[16] On Semi-Pelagianism see Pelikan, *The Christian Tradition*, vol. 1, 319–24.

What is of additional importance here is that Augustine and Prosper might not be appealing only to prayer in general in support of their common theological position but to a particular widely known intercessory prayer of the liturgy. That is, because Augustine refers to prayer for unbelievers, catechumens, and faithful, and Prosper to similar groups, as well as to Jews, schismatics, heretics, the lapsed, enemies of the cross of Christ, and idolaters, it has often been assumed that the liturgical prayer in question is a version of the solemn intercessions of the Good Friday liturgy in the Roman Church, such as is clearly present in the liturgy by the seventh-century *Gelasian Sacramentary*.[17] If so, then this would actually help us in dating these prayers rather early in the church's history, at least to the fifth century.

Alternatively, however, De Clerck is undoubtedly correct in noting that several of the categories of people for whom prayer is made, according to Prosper's text, do not appear in the Good Friday solemn prayers and that one cannot automatically conclude that it is to such a prayer that he is referring. Rather, it is to intercessory prayer for grace in general, made on behalf of diverse groups of people in the liturgy, and not to that specific Good Friday prayer, which, even if present in fifth-century Rome was not necessarily known or used elsewhere in the Christian West in that time period.

Whatever intercessory liturgical prayer either Augustine or Prosper knew in the liturgies of their day, the principle of *ut legem credendi lex statuat supplicandi* is a principle about the supplication for grace and the priority of grace in the *ordo salutis* (order of salvation). Hence, in the first historical use of this phrase, summarized by *lex orandi, lex credendi*, the issue is soteriology, how human beings are saved. And the way the church prays to God reveals that the answer is divine grace at the beginning, middle, and end. Such an Augustinian theology defended by Prosper and others will come to be enshrined in the twenty-five canons of a local Gallican council, the Council of Orange in 529 CE, which, through ratification by Pope Boniface II in 531, became part of accepted doctrine in Western Christianity. Here, one thousand years before the sixteenth-century Protestant and

---

[17] *Liber Sacramentorum Romanae Aeclesiae Ordinis Anni Circuli (Cod. Vat. Reg. lat. 316/Paris Bibl. Nat. 7193, 41/56 Sacramentarium Gelasianum)*, ed. L.C. Mohlberg (Rome: Herder, 1960), 64–67.

Catholic reformations is what Western Christianity said about grace and salvation, a theological-doctrinal position supported, as we have seen, by the *lex orandi*:

The Canons of the Council of Orange (529 AD)[18]
CANON 1. If anyone denies that it is the whole man, that is, both body and soul, that was "changed for the worse" through the offense of Adam's sin, but believes that the freedom of the soul remains unimpaired and that only the body is subject to corruption, he is deceived by the error of Pelagius and contradicts the scripture which says, "The soul that sins shall die" (Ezek. 18:20); and, "Do you not know that if you yield yourselves to anyone as obedient slaves, you are the slaves of the one whom you obey?" (Rom. 6:16); and, "For whatever overcomes a man, to that he is enslaved" (2 Pet. 2:19).

CANON 2. If anyone asserts that Adam's sin affected him alone and not his descendants also, or at least if he declares that it is only the death of the body which is the punishment for sin, and not also that sin, which is the death of the soul, passed through one man to the whole human race, he does injustice to God and contradicts the Apostle, who says, "Therefore as sin came into the world through one man and death through sin, and so death spread to all men because all men sinned" (Rom. 5:12).

CANON 3. If anyone says that the grace of God can be conferred as a result of human prayer, but that it is not grace itself which makes us pray to God, he contradicts the prophet Isaiah, or the Apostle who says the same thing, "I have been found by those who did not seek me; I have shown myself to those who did not ask for me" (Rom 10:20, quoting Isa. 65:1).

CANON 4. If anyone maintains that God awaits our will to be cleansed from sin, but does not confess that even our will to be cleansed comes to us through the infusion and working of the Holy Spirit, he resists the Holy Spirit himself who says through Solomon, "The will is prepared by the Lord" (Prov. 8:35, LXX), and the salutary word of the Apostle, "For God is at work in you, both to will and to work for his good pleasure" (Phil. 2:13).

---

[18] H. Denzinger, *Enchridion Symbolorum* (Freiburg: Herder, 1955), 85–92. This translation from the Center for Reformed Theology and Apologetics, Online Resource, http://www.reformed.org/index.html. Used by permission.

CANON 5. If anyone says that not only the increase of faith but also its beginning and the very desire for faith, by which we believe in Him who justifies the ungodly and comes to the regeneration of holy baptism—if anyone says that this belongs to us by nature and not by a gift of grace, that is, by the inspiration of the Holy Spirit amending our will and turning it from unbelief to faith and from godlessness to godliness, it is proof that he is opposed to the teaching of the Apostles, for blessed Paul says, "And I am sure that he who began a good work in you will bring it to completion at the day of Jesus Christ" (Phil. 1:6). And again, "For by grace you have been saved through faith; and this is not your own doing, it is the gift of God" (Eph. 2:8). For those who state that the faith by which we believe in God is natural make all who are separated from the Church of Christ by definition in some measure believers.

CANON 6. If anyone says that God has mercy upon us when, apart from his grace, we believe, will, desire, strive, labor, pray, watch, study, seek, ask, or knock, but does not confess that it is by the infusion and inspiration of the Holy Spirit within us that we have the faith, the will, or the strength to do all these things as we ought; or if anyone makes the assistance of grace depend on the humility or obedience of man and does not agree that it is a gift of grace itself that we are obedient and humble, he contradicts the Apostle who says, "What have you that you did not receive?" (1 Cor. 4:7), and, "But by the grace of God I am what I am" (1 Cor. 15:10).

CANON 7. If anyone affirms that we can form any right opinion or make any right choice which relates to the salvation of eternal life, as is expedient for us, or that we can be saved, that is, assent to the preaching of the gospel through our natural powers without the illumination and inspiration of the Holy Spirit, who makes all men gladly assent to and believe in the truth, he is led astray by a heretical spirit, and does not understand the voice of God who says in the Gospel, "For apart from me you can do nothing" (John 15:5), and the word of the Apostle, "Not that we are competent of ourselves to claim anything as coming from us; our competence is from God" (2 Cor. 3:5).

CANON 8. If anyone maintains that some are able to come to the grace of baptism by mercy but others through free will, which has manifestly been corrupted in all those who have been born after the transgression of the first man, it is proof that he has no place in the true faith. For he denies that the free will of all men has been weakened through the sin of the first man, or at least holds that it has been affected in such a way that they have still the ability to seek the mystery of eternal salvation by themselves without the revelation of God. The Lord himself shows how contradictory this is by declaring that no one is able to come to him "unless the Father who sent me draws him" (John 6:44), as he also says to Peter, "Blessed are you, Simon Bar-Jona! For flesh and blood has not revealed this to you, but my Father who is in heaven" (Matt. 16:17), and as the Apostle says, "No one can say 'Jesus is Lord' except by the Holy Spirit" (1 Cor. 12:3).

CANON 9. Concerning the succor of God. It is a mark of divine favor when we are of a right purpose and keep our feet from hypocrisy and unrighteousness; for as often as we do good, God is at work in us and with us, in order that we may do so.

CANON 10. Concerning the succor of God. The succor of God is to be ever sought by the regenerate and converted also, so that they may be able to come to a successful end or persevere in good works.

CANON 11. Concerning the duty to pray. None would make any true prayer to the Lord had he not received from him the object of his prayer, as it is written, "Of thy own have we given thee" (1 Chron. 29:14).

CANON 12. Of what sort we are whom God loves. God loves us for what we shall be by his gift, and not by our own deserving.

CANON 13. Concerning the restoration of free will. The freedom of will that was destroyed in the first man can be restored only by the grace of baptism, for what is lost can be returned only by the one who was able to give it. Hence the Truth itself declares: "So if the Son makes you free, you will be free indeed" (John 8:36).

CANON 14. No mean wretch is freed from his sorrowful state, however great it may be, save the one who is anticipated by the mercy of God, as the Psalmist says, "Let thy compassion come speedily to meet us" (Ps. 79:8), and again, "My God in his steadfast love will meet me" (Ps. 59:10).

CANON 15. Adam was changed, but for the worse, through his own iniquity from what God made him. Through the grace of God the believer is changed, but for the better, from what his iniquity has done for him. The one, therefore, was the change brought about by the first sinner; the other, according to the Psalmist, is the change of the right hand of the Most High (Ps. 77:10).

CANON 16. No man shall be honored by his seeming attainment, as though it were not a gift, or suppose that he has received it because a missive from without stated it in writing or in speech. For the Apostle speaks thus, "For if justification were through the law, then Christ died to no purpose" (Gal. 2:21); and "When he ascended on high he led a host of captives, and he gave gifts to men" (Eph. 4:8, quoting Ps. 68:18). It is from this source that any man has what he does; but whoever denies that he has it from this source either does not truly have it, or else "even what he has will be taken away" (Matt. 25:29).

CANON 17. Concerning Christian courage. The courage of the Gentiles is produced by simple greed, but the courage of Christians by the love of God which "has been poured into our hearts" not by freedom of will from our own side but "through the Holy Spirit which has been given to us" (Rom. 5:5).

CANON 18. That grace is not preceded by merit. Recompense is due to good works if they are performed; but grace, to which we have no claim, precedes them, to enable them to be done.

CANON 19. That a man can be saved only when God shows mercy. Human nature, even though it remained in that sound state in which it was created, could by no means save itself, without the assistance of the Creator; hence since man cannot safe-guard his salvation without the grace of God, which is a gift, how will he be able to restore what he has lost without the grace of God?

CANON 20. That a man can do no good without God. God does much that is good in a man that the man does not do; but a man does nothing good for which God is not responsible, so as to let him do it.

CANON 21. Concerning nature and grace. As the Apostle most truly says to those who would be justified by the law and have fallen from grace, "If justification were through the law, then Christ died to no purpose" (Gal. 2:21), so it is most truly declared to those who imagine that grace, which faith in Christ advocates and lays hold of, is nature: "If justification were through nature, then Christ died to no purpose." Now there was indeed the law, but it did not justify, and there was indeed nature, but it did not justify. Not in vain did Christ therefore die, so that the law might be fulfilled by him who said, "I have come not to abolish them, but to fulfil them" (Matt. 5:17), and that the nature which had been destroyed by Adam might be restored by him who said that he had come "to seek and to save the lost" (Luke 19:10).

CANON 22. Concerning those things that belong to man. No man has anything of his own but untruth and sin. But if a man has any truth or righteousness, it is from that fountain for which we must thirst in this desert, so that we may be refreshed from it as by drops of water and not faint on the way.

CANON 23. Concerning the will of God and of man. Men do their own will and not the will of God when they do what displeases him; but when they follow their own will and comply with the will of God, however willingly they do so, yet it is his will by which what they will is both prepared and instructed.

CANON 24. Concerning the branches of the vine. The branches on the vine do not give life to the vine, but receive life from it; thus the vine is related to its branches in such a way that it supplies them with what they need to live, and does not take this from them. Thus it is to the advantage of the disciples, not Christ, both to have Christ abiding in them and to abide in Christ. For if the vine is cut down another can shoot up from the live root; but one who is cut off from the vine cannot live without the root (John 15:5ff).

CANON 25. Concerning the love with which we love God. It is wholly a gift of God to love God. He who loves, even though he is not loved, allowed himself to be loved. We are loved, even when we displease him, so that we might have means to please him. For the Spirit, whom we love with the Father and the Son, has poured into our hearts the love of the Father and the Son (Rom. 5:5).

Salvation by the grace of God—even by faith (canon 5)—is, in part at least, a *liturgical* doctrine!

2. The *Lex Orandi*: Not a Principle in Isolation from Others

Liturgical prayer is for neither Augustine nor Prosper the only doctrinal source they use in their arguments, and it is not even the primary one. In the context of his response to Pelagianism and the development of his theology of original sin and grace, Augustine is also trying to be a faithful interpreter of Scripture, in this case, Paul in Romans 5:12: "as sin came into the world through one man, and death came through sin, . . . so death spread to all because all have sinned." Similarly, Prosper himself indicates that liturgical prayer, the *lex supplicandi*, is but one of *several* sources he uses in this defense of the necessity of divine grace. Nevertheless, contemporary liturgical theologians often approach the *lex orandi* as though it is the foundational, primary, or most important theological source. Aidan Kavanagh, for example, says that:

Lex supplicandi is something much more specific than the broad and fuzzy notion of the "practice of the Church". . . . It is a law of supplicatory prayer—not prayer or worship in general, but of prayer which petitions God for the whole range of human needs in spec, a law of euchological petition. This is the nub of the reason why the *lex supplicandi* founds and constitutes the *lex credendi* and is therefore primary for Christian theology. The way Christians believe is, somehow, constituted and supported by how Christians petition God for their human needs in worship.[19]

But is this what Prosper actually says? It appears that Prosper's use of this principle is but *another* argument against semi-Pelagianism made by him *in addition to* one based on the "inviolable decrees of the blessed apostolic see." Furthermore, it seems quite clear that what gives the *lex orandi* any authority whatsoever in this context is that (1) this "sacred testimony of priestly intercessions" has been, in Prosper's opinion, "transmitted from the apostles themselves" and (2) these intercessions are "uniformly celebrated throughout the world and in every catholic church." Hence, the *lex supplicandi* can also be said to "constitute" the *lex credendi*, but not as an isolated norm or principle. Rather, it can function in this way because it conforms to the traditional and biblical *doctrinal* teaching of the church. In other words, Prosper's argument is a doctrinal one, which uses liturgical evidence in addition to other evidence because that liturgical evidence is consistent with and illustrative of those other sources, namely, Scripture and Tradition. Hence, what Prosper also does *not* say is that one of these sources is more important—or more foundational—than the other. Instead, as Paul Marshall has written correctly:

> Despite the romantic attachment many in the field of liturgical studies may have for it, it is necessary to demythologize *"lex orandi."* . . . Prosper's dictum has become the basis of a kind of fundamentalism. Rather too many writers strip the original *ut legem credendi lex statuat supplicandi* of *"ut"* and ignore the function of *statuat* as the subjunctive of *statuere*, and so read the dictum as though it were an axiom. Thus the dictum evolved into the simplistic equation, *lex orandi lex credendi*, and liturgical material is employed in a . . . hierarchical and sometimes authoritarian manner. . . . In the out-of-context form in which we usually find them, Prosper's words are used to establish for liturgy a doctrinal authority that he would never have

[19] Kavanagh, *On Liturgical Theology* (New York: Pueblo, 1984), 134.

recognized. . . . Most of his writing . . . takes the form of explication of scripture and recollection of apostolic and sub-apostolic testimony. In the entirety of his work, he uses liturgical evidence in only three places, but never as his first line of reasoning and never as the basis for his larger claims. . . . [H]e mounts all the evidence he knows to assert that believing is a gift of God.[20]

Two things, therefore, must be said about what Marshall calls this "dictum." First, the dictum refers to the *lex supplicandi* as *a* source for *doctrine*. And, second, the *lex supplicandi* can be considered as *a* source not because it is independent or somehow foundational or primary but because the content of the liturgical prayer to which Prosper refers is already shaped, formed, and constituted in agreement with Scripture and Tradition. De Clerk concludes in a similar manner about the original sense and meaning of Prosper's phrase:

> To determine what the rule of faith is, it is necessary . . . to refer to the content of the prayer of the Church, to its formulation. But it is important to point out that in the mind of the monk from Acquitaine . . . the liturgical formulas have value as a theological argument only insofar as they are founded on scripture and attested by tradition. In other words . . . what is said in prayer is credited with theological value to the degree that it is based on biblical revelation as the universal Church understands it. Prosper does not oppose Bible and liturgy, any more than he separates liturgy and tradition. In his mind, one may have recourse to the prayers of the Church in order to resolve the controversy on grace because they correspond to a biblical mandate [1 Tim 2:1-2], and are the expression of the living tradition of the Church. Such is the significance of the phrase *ut legem credendi lex statuat supplicandi*, seen in its context.[21]

More recently, liturgical historian Paul Bradshaw has entered into this conversation. Bradshaw also looks critically at the use of the Latin formula *lex orandi, lex credendi* in liturgical theology in the original and classic sense of the relationship between liturgy and *doctrine* as described above. Hence, Bradshaw argues that this Latin phrase should

---

[20] Paul Marshall, "Reconsidering 'Liturgical Theology': Is There a *Lex Orandi* for All Christians?," *Studia Liturgica* 25 (1995): 139–40.

[21] De Clerck, "'Lex orandi, lex credendi': The Original Sense," 192.

not be used as a kind of liturgical "proof text" in liturgical theology. That is, one should not invoke this principle in order to "determine . . . *a priori* what doctrinal position one espouses, and then quarrie . . . ancient liturgical texts in order to find material that could be interpreted in support of that position, sometimes without regard for the history of the text in question or its broader context in the rite."[22] He notes, similarly, that the use of this phrase has been "highly selective," with "certain features of liturgical practice . . . highlighted as authentic, while others are disregarded as aberrations from the norm."[23] As examples of this selective approach, he points to the fact that although modern liturgical reform has given a theological priority to the early Christian period in general, it has not always regarded several equally evidenced liturgical practices or interpretations as having equal weight for the renewal of the church's worship today (e.g., episcopal elections by the people and the abandonment of other baptismal rites and images in favor of the "paschal mystery" priority of Romans 6). Although the claim is often made in such contexts that the liturgy itself is the "source" for Christian theology, doctrine, and/or renewal, the fact of the matter is that doctrine itself tends to shape not only liturgy but how people actually "read" liturgical texts and practice. In his words, *lex orandi, lex credendi* is "always a two-way street."[24] That is, as we shall see in more detail below in chapter 5, the *lex credendi*, in this case what the church believes, teaches, and confesses, also shapes what and how it prays. Edward Kilmartin expresses this relationship well:

> The slogan "law of prayer–law of belief" leaves in suspense which magnitude might be the subject, and which the predicate, in particular instances. Consequently, it seems legitimate to state the axiom in this way: *the law of prayer is the law of belief, and vice versa.* . . . On the one hand, the law of prayer implies a comprehensive, and, in some measure a pre-reflective, perception of the life of faith. On the other hand, the law of belief must be introduced because the question of the value of a particular liturgical tradition requires the employment of theoretical discourse. One must reckon with the limits of the liturgy

[22] Paul Bradshaw, "Difficulties in Doing Liturgical Theology," *Pacifica* 11 (June 1998): 187.

[23] Ibid.

[24] Ibid., 188.

as lived practice of the faith. History has taught us that forms of liturgical prayer and ritual activity, however orthodox, often had to be dropped or changed to avoid heretical misunderstanding. Moreover, in new historical and cultural situations, the question of the correspondence between the community's understanding of Christian truth, and its expression in the liturgy and that of the authentic whole tradition, must continually be placed. To respond responsibly to this problem, other sources of theology must be introduced along with the liturgical-practical grounding of the knowledge of faith.[25]

In addition, Bradshaw offers a strong critique of Aidan Kavanagh's popular methodological distinction between *theologia prima*, based on the liturgical assembly's direct liturgical experience, and *theologia secunda*, arising from secondary theological reflection upon that experience.[26] "Even if we were to grant the premise . . . that it is possible to distinguish primary theology from secondary reflection," notes Bradshaw, "the problem is not thereby resolved." He continues:

> Those who are the strongest advocates of the theory that it is the natural piety of worshippers that should be accorded the most significant weight in liturgical theology are the ones most likely to be unhappy if this were to be put into practice. Aidan Kavanagh's writings have introduced his readers to the figure of "Mrs Murphy," who represents the ordinary person in the pew and who is therefore understood to be the authentic exponent of "primary theology." . . . [But], it is precisely the expressions of natural piety of the putative Mrs Murphy and countless other churchgoers—devotions to the sacred heart of Jesus, for example, or sentimental nineteenth-century hymns—that are usually denigrated by the professional liturgical theologian and swept away by the liturgical reformer on the grounds that they fail to conform to the inherent spirit of the liturgy! Where is the value attached to *theologia prima* here?[27]

The liturgy that is actually experienced in Christian assemblies has itself also been shaped and conditioned by several factors—doctrinal,

---

[25] Edward Kilmartin, *Christian Liturgy: Theology and Practice*, vol. 1: *Systematic Theology* (Kansas City: Sheed & Ward, 1988), 97.

[26] See Kavangh's *On Liturgical Theology*, passim.

[27] Bradshaw, "Difficulties," 192–93.

canonical, and catechetical—all three of which are the products of *theologia secunda*, according to Kavanagh's categories.

3. The Continued Importance of the *Lex Supplicandi* for Doctrine

Because the famous phrase of Prosper as presented above turns out to be a rather limited argument with reference specifically to the development of doctrine, there are those today who would question the continued appropriateness of its use for and within liturgical theology itself. Both Paul Marshall and Michael Aune are within this camp, with Marshall, as we have seen, calling for the "demythologizing" of the *lex orandi, lex credendi* approach, an approach to theology often taken out of its original sense and context. Aune goes a step further than Marshall here and calls for the "retirement" of this dictum altogether, writing:

> In fact, it is time to set aside Prosper's dictum as the *locus classicus* of primary theology or of liturgical theologies that have been pursued up to this juncture and to find, instead, a different starting place from which to understand liturgy and its relationship with theology.[28]

Because of the way it is often used, even as a "proof text" in theological discourse, I do have some sympathies with Aune, although I much prefer here Marshall's suggestion of "demythologizing" the dictum rather than abandoning it altogether in the theological process. That is, properly understood as referring to one source among others, it is still a meaningful phrase underscoring the importance of the church's liturgies for coming to articulate and understand the church's theology of God, the divine initiative taken in salvation, and the historic orthodox faith of the church. Here I must confess that I am still somewhat taken with Alexander Schmemann's basic approach to the question, which is much less speculative about liturgy or theology than the approaches of many of his disciples have been.

As is well known, Schmemann devoted a number of his writings to the question of the relationship between liturgy and theology.[29]

---

[28] Aune, "Liturgy and Theology: Rethinking the Relationship, Part 1, Setting the Stage," *Worship* 81, no. 1 (January 2007): 68.

[29] See his *Introduction to Liturgical Theology*, 2nd ed. (Crestwood, NY: St. Vladimir's Seminary Press, 1975); *For the Life of the World* (Crestwood, NY: St.

According to him, neither "liturgical theology" as a subdiscipline within the broader theological curriculum nor the attempt to develop a "theology of liturgy" from which one might deduce the correct norms to which a program of liturgical reform must conform are adequate approaches to this question. Rather, theology as the "orderly and consistent presentation, explication and defense of the Church's faith" must be rooted in the very experience of the faith itself, an experience that is "given and received in the Church's *leitourgia*—in her lex *orandi*."[30] In other words, for Schmemann the *lex orandi is* (*est*) the church's *lex credendi*, and the theological task is ultimately an interpretative and descriptive process that attempts "to grasp the 'theology' as revealed in and through liturgy."[31] He maintains that if theology is

> the attempt to express Truth itself, to find words adequate to the mind and experience of the Church, then it must of necessity have its source where the faith, the mind, and the experience of the Church have their living focus and expression, where faith in both essential meanings of that word, as Truth revealed and given, and as Truth accepted and "lived," has its *epiphany*, and that is precisely the function of the "*leitourgia*."[32]

For Schmemann, there is therefore no need for specific kinds of theology called either "liturgical theology" or "theology of liturgy." Although theology should not be reduced to liturgy, all Christian theology should somehow be "liturgical," in that it has "its ultimate term of reference in the faith of the Church, as manifested and communicated in the liturgy."[33] And it is within the liturgy above all that

---

Vladimir's Seminary Press, 1973); "Liturgical Theology, Theology of Liturgy, and Liturgical Reform," *St. Vladimir's Theological Quarterly* (1969): 217–24; and "Liturgy and Theology," *The Greek Orthodox Theological Review* 17 (1972): 86–100. See also, *Liturgy and Tradition: Theological Reflections of Alexander Schmemann*, ed. Thomas Fisch (Crestwood, NY: St. Vladimir's Seminary Press, 1990).

[30] Schmemann, "Liturgy and Theology," 89–90.

[31] Schmemann, "Liturgical Theology, Theology of Liturgy, and Liturgical Reform," 218.

[32] Ibid., 219.

[33] Schmemann, "Liturgy and Theology," 95.

the Church is *informed* of her cosmical and eschatological vocation, *receives* the power to fulfill it and thus truly *becomes* "what she is"— the sacrament, in Christ, of the Kingdom. In this sense the liturgy is indeed "means of grace" . . . in the all-embracing meaning as the means of always making the Church what she is—a realm of grace, of communion with God, of new knowledge and new life. The liturgy of the Church is cosmical and eschatological because the Church is cosmical and eschatological; but the Church would not have been cosmical and eschatological had she not been given, as the very source and constitution of her life and faith, the *experience* of the new creation, the experience and vision of the Kingdom which is to come. And this is precisely the "leitourgia" of the Church's cult, the function which makes it the source and indeed the very possibility of theology.[34]

Because, according to Schmemann, the church's *lex orandi is* the church's true *lex credendi*, the task of theology is to explicate, explain, and defend this liturgically received vision and experience. Hence, for him, the church's faith is revealed and expressed and so becomes the "source" for theological reflection and discourse, even if that discourse is limited to the explanation, explication, and defense of that "liturgical" vision.

It might certainly be argued here that on one level this is exactly what Prosper was trying to do, namely, to explicate and defend liturgically the faith of the church as it is related to the primacy and priority of grace in the process of salvation. That is, what Prosper articulates here does have "its ultimate term of reference in the faith of the Church, as manifested and communicated in the liturgy."

Where Schmemann departs from or goes beyond Prosper, however, is in his apparent limiting of the experience of God's salvation to *the leitourgia* of the church as *the* source in isolation from other sources of grace and faith. But, as Robert Taft has written:

Liturgy in the narrower sense of the word—actual Christian liturgies, worship services, the liturgical celebration—is *one privileged ground* of this divine encounter, *one theophany or revelation* of God's saving presence among us in the world today. It is by no means the only

---

[34] Ibid., 92.

ground of this encounter, however, for God does not depend on our liturgy to meet us and call us to him.[35]

And, as he states further:

Basic to all presences of the Risen Christ in his Church is his presence in faith. Prior to faith is the presence of the Spirit, however. For faith is rooted in the action of the Spirit, which makes faith possible and through which Christ is present.[36]

Indeed, as I have argued elsewhere with specific reference to Kavanagh's interpretation of liturgy as "primary theology" approach:

[O]ne is led to ask whether there is not something else which is even more primary than this liturgical act, some kind of *lex credendi* perhaps which comes to expression in, is continually nourished by, but, nevertheless, in some fundamental primordial way "constitutes" the *lex orandi.* And might not this "something else" be the living address of the Word of God spoken and responded to in faith, which is indeed present in, experienced by, and celebrated in the liturgical act, but in no way bound to that act but bound instead to the Spirit of God?[37]

Nevertheless, Schmemann's overall approach remains, in my opinion, a most helpful approach to the question of the relationship between liturgy and doctrine. Indeed, *lex orandi [est] lex credendi* reminds us that what the church believes, teaches, and confesses will certainly be reflected and expressed within its worship. Consequently, if one wants to understand a particular religious tradition, one must not only read its theological or doctrinal texts but also experience and consciously study its worship. Again, it is Taft who, in citing Gerhard Delling, summarizes the value in this approach, writing:

"Worship is the self-portrayal of religion. In worship the sources by which religion lives are made visible, its expectations and hopes are

---

[35] Robert Taft, "What Does Liturgy Do? Toward a Theology of Liturgical Celebration: Some Theses," in *Beyond East and West: Problems in Liturgical Understanding,* 2nd rev. and enlarged ed. (Rome: Pontificio Istituto Orientale, 1997), 242.

[36] Ibid., 250.

[37] Maxwell E. Johnson, "Liturgy and Theology," in *Worship: Rites, Feasts, and Reflections* (Portland: Pastoral Press, 2004), 321.

expressed, and the forces which sustain it are made known. In many respects the essence of a religion is more directly intelligible in its worship than in statements of its basic principles or even in descriptions of its sentiments." What Delling says here on the phenomenological/ epistemological level is even more true on the existential: not only in worship is religion *known*; it is through worship that it is *fed and lives.*[38]

Therefore, ongoing participation in the liturgical experience continues to be formative of faith and life for those already initiated into Christ and the church. For those outside, however, at least in early Christianity, worship did not and could not function as a tool for evangelism and conversion. That is, people did not become Christian because they somehow experienced "the new creation, the experience and vision of the Kingdom which is to come" in the church's worship. Rather, as Mennonite author Alan Kreider has recently said of worship in the early church:

> Christian worship was designed to enable *Christians* to worship God. *It was not designed to attract non-Christians*; it was *not "seeker-sensitive."* For seekers were not allowed in. . . . Christian worship . . . assisted in the outreach of the churches indirectly, as a by-product, by shaping the lives and character of individual Christians and their communities so that they would be intriguing.[39]

What was available for others who found Christianity "intriguing" was the catechumenate, which, by the end of the fourth century, focused not only on moral formation and discipleship but clearly on doctrine as well.

4. Conclusion

As noted in the introduction to this work, my goal in this study is not to attempt a resolution of the various approaches taken today in the discipline of liturgical theology. What I have been concerned with in this chapter is nothing other than trying to understand the

---

[38] Taft, "What Does Liturgy Do?," 255–56.

[39] Alan Kreider, *The Change of Conversion and the Origin of Christendom* (Harrisburg, PA: Trinity Press International, 1999), 14.

applicability and limits of the phrase, dictum, adage, or axiom of Prosper of Aquitaine, *"ut legem credendi lex statuat supplicandi,"* in its historical context. What we have seen is that the appeal of Prosper to the church's supplicatory prayer for divine grace for a variety of people and needs was but one of several arguments used by him to combat semi-Pelagianism. What this means is that the entire phrase, or its abbreviated form, *"lex orandi, lex credendi,"* has as its point of reference the doctrine of the church, in this particular case, the doctrine of salvation by the grace of God. One might be even more specific here and say that the phrase originally had nothing to do specifically with the discipline of "theology" at all but rather with the role of liturgical prayer in bearing and expressing what was already determined to be the orthodox faith of the church with relation to its doctrine of grace. Yes, Prosper was reflecting theologically on Scripture, Tradition, and the content and experience of the church at prayer, but he was not taking the liturgical principle out of context as some sort of independent "proof text."

Nevertheless, interpreted in the way of Prosper himself, as but one source among others, but also as a source that is continually experienced over and over again by the members of the church in their liturgical convocations, liturgical prayer does have a privileged place in the formation, development, and expression of doctrine. It is to this we turn in the next two chapters dealing with specific trinitarian and christological doctrine.

Chapter 2

Doxology and Trinity

In the limited but historically accurate sense that the principle *"ut legem credendi lex statuat supplicandi"* was defined in the previous chapter, that is, in service to the orthodox Christian doctrine of grace, so in relationship to the early development and articulation of orthodox Christian faith in God as Trinity does liturgical prayer play a similar and important role. Nonetheless, it must be noted from the beginning that no one in the fourth or fifth century appeals to a theoretical *principle* like that articulated by Prosper in the sixth century in support of this. Appeals to worship and its practices, yes, but no appeals to anything approximating something called the *lex orandi*, since the adage had not yet been developed!

This chapter proceeds by looking first at the tradition of prayer to Christ, both liturgical and otherwise, as that leads, at least, to an overall context that would foster the logic of the relationship between the Son and the Father as *homoousios* or *consubstantial* in the first phase of the development of the Nicene Creed at the Council of Nicea (325 CE). The way in which the divine role of the Spirit in the liturgical acts, rites, and doxologies of the church and elsewhere is appealed to after Nicea in defense of the equality of the Holy Spirit to the Father and Son at the Council of Constantinople (381 CE) will form the second part. As will be seen, just as the liturgical-sacramental rite of baptism tended to play a role in resolving the semi-Pelagian controversy, so does it, together with the Eucharist and its liturgy, come to play a very important role already in this earlier context. Indeed, praying plays a formative role in the development of classic trinitarian Christian doctrine and faith.

1. Prayer to Christ and the Nicene *Homoousios*

What became the orthodox Christian understanding of the relationship between God the Son and God the Father at the Council of

Nicea in 325 is expressed in the second article or section of what is now called the Nicene-Constantinopolitan Creed:

> And in one Lord Jesus Christ, the only-begotten Son of God,
> Begotten from the Father before all time,
> Light from Light, true God from true God,
> begotten not created,
> of the same essence [reality] as the Father [*homoousion to patri*],
> through Whom all things came into being.[1]

How does the worship of Christ contribute to this profession of *homoousios*? How, again, does prayer assist in shaping believing? It is this that concerns us in what follows.

Thanks in large part to Joseph Jungmann's classic study, *The Place of Christ in Liturgical Prayer*,[2] traditional scholarship on prayer has tended to take Origen of Alexandria's following description as the normative Christian definition of how prayer is to be offered:

> Now if we are to take prayer in its most exact sense, perhaps we should not pray to anyone begotten, not even to Christ Himself, but only to the God and Father of all, to whom even our Savior Himself prayed . . . and to whom He taught us to pray. For when He heard, "teach us to pray," He did not teach us to pray to Himself, but to the Father by saying "Our Father in heaven, and so forth" (Lk. 11:1ff.; Mt. 6:5ff.). . . . Consequently . . . we should pray only to the God and Father of all, yet not without the High Priest, who was appointed "with an oath" according to the verse, "He has sworn and will not change His mind, You are a priest forever after the order of Melchisedek" (Ps. 110:4; Heb. 7:20-21).[3]

Hence, for Jungmann, classic Christian prayer before Nicea, especially when offered officially in public, was always *to* God, *through*

---

[1] Translation adapted from *Creeds of the Churches: A Reader in Christian Doctrine from the Bible to the Present*, trans. John H. Leith, 3rd ed. (Louisville: Westminster / John Knox Press, 1982), 33.

[2] Josef Jungmann, *The Place of Christ in Liturgical Prayer* (Collegeville, MN: Liturgical Press, 1989).

[3] Origen, *On Prayer*, 15.1. Translated from *Origen: An Exhortation to Martyrdom, Prayer and Selected Works*, trans. Rowan A. Greer, The Classics of Western Spirituality (New York: Paulist Press, 1979), 112–13.

Christ the High Priest and Mediator (see 1 Tim 2:5), *in* the Holy Spirit. While variations did exist, with prayer directly *to* Christ well known from several sources, these were often relegated to the sidelines by Jungmann as aberrations, evidence of popular devotion and piety, or the idiosyncratic deviations of particular heretical movements on the fringes of orthodox Christianity. It was, according to Jungmann, the *homoousios* of Nicea in the context of Arianism and the Council of Constantinople in the context of semi-Arianism—and its after-math—that would lead to liturgical prayer losing the active sense of Christ as priest and mediator in his humanity and so now being made directly *to* Christ in the liturgy as well as lead to addressing liturgical prayer directly to all three persons of the Trinity at once. For Jungmann, such would open the way for new forms of human mediation now associated with Mary and the saints, especially in medieval Western Christianity.[4]

The way of reading those "alternative" liturgical sources dismissed by Jungmann, however, has changed dramatically since his time. In February 2005, an international scholarly conference was held at the Yale Institute of Sacred Music and Yale Divinity School under the deliberately chosen title *The Place of Christ in Liturgical Prayer: Trinity, Christology, and Liturgical Theology.*[5] Three of the papers presented at this conference have a direct bearing on the focus of this chapter: Bryan Spinks, "The Place of Christ in Liturgical Prayer: What Jung-mann Omitted to Say";[6] Larry W. Hurtado, "The Binitarian Pattern of Earliest Christian Devotion and Early Doctrinal Development";[7] and Paul Bradshaw, "God, Christ, and the Holy Spirit in Early Chris-tian Praying."[8] All three of these essays challenge Jungmann's too

[4] Josef Jungmann, "The Defeat of Teutonic Arianism and the Revolution in Religious Culture in the Early Middle Ages," in idem, *Pastoral Liturgy* (New York: Herder and Herder, 1962), 1–101.

[5] Bryan D. Spinks, ed., *The Place of Christ in Liturgical Prayer: Trinity, Christology, and Liturgical Theology* (Collegeville, MN: Liturgical Press, Pueblo, 2008).

[6] Bryan Spinks, "The Place of Christ in Liturgical Prayer: What Jungmann Omitted to Say," in ibid., 1–20.

[7] Larry W. Hurtado, "The Binitarian Pattern of Earliest Christian Devotion and Early Doctrinal Development," in ibid., 23–50.

[8] Paul Bradshaw, "God, Christ, and the Holy Spirit in Early Christian Praying," in ibid., 51–64.

easy omission of other sources as nonauthoritative and demonstrate that the picture of early Christian prayer—even liturgical prayer—to Christ is far more widespread and formative than previously assumed.

Further, it was often the case in the past that theologians, historians, and, perhaps especially, liturgiologists tended to denigrate or even dismiss what is often (even pejoratively) called "popular religion" as but "superstition," vestiges of "paganism," or as reflecting, somehow, a "lower" form of belief and practice among the "unenlightened" than the "official religion" of the elite. Modern scholarship, however, has been more willing to embrace a much broader view of the whole, including the religious lives and practices of the poor, women, and others as theological and liturgical "sources." Peter Brown's important 1981 work, *The Cult of the Saints: Its Rise and Function in Latin Christianity*, represents a significant scholarly shift in this context. Here, in particular, Brown argues convincingly that the *real* history of the early church is to be read, precisely, in the development of the "popular" practices and beliefs associated with the cult of the martyrs and later saints at their shrines in the overall shaping of late antique culture, religion, and society, practices shared by both the intellectually elite and others in the church, in spite of their differing intellectual facilities.[9] And, on a similar note, in the 2004 *Festschrift* for Paul Bradshaw, Robert Taft writes of the turn his own work has taken, saying, "In so doing I have, in a sense, been responding to my own appeal, made years ago, that we 'integrate into our work the methods of the relatively recent *pietá popolare* or *annales* schools of Christian history in Europe' and study liturgy not just from the top down, i.e., in its official or semi-official texts, but also from the bottom up, 'as something real people did.'"[10] In the first two centuries, in fact, the lines between "official" public prayer and "private" prayer are not

---

[9] Peter Brown, *The Cult of the Saints: Its Rise and Function in Latin Christianity* (Chicago: University of Chicago Press, 1981), 12ff. See, more recently, Candida Moss, *The Other Christs: Imitating Jesus in Ancient Christian Ideologies of Martyrdom* (New York: Oxford Publishing House, 2010).

[10] Robert F. Taft, "The Order and Place of Lay Communion in the Late Antique and Byzantine East," in *Studia Liturgica Diversa: Essays in Honor of Paul F. Bradshaw*, ed. Maxwell E. Johnson and L. Edward Phillips (Portland: Pastoral Press, 2004), 130.

all that clear, especially because, as Bradshaw notes,[11] most prayer and worship happened in domestic settings.

One of the major contributions to the development and interpretation of Christology as formed in part by prayer and devotion at the earliest stages of Christianity is the work of New Testament scholar Larry W. Hurtado. In several of his works[12] Hurtado argues that the worship of Christ as divine—as God—was not the result of a christological evolution in thought shaping this kind of conclusion only in the later writings of the New Testament (e.g., in the Gospel of John) but already a common reality even in the time of the early letters of St. Paul. Nor was such worship of Christ the result of Greco-Roman pagan influence on the early Christian communities moving from Judaism into a Gentile context. Rather:

> the origins of the worship of Jesus are so early that practically any evolutionary approach is rendered invalid as historical explanation. Our earliest Christian writings, from approximately 50–60 C.E., already presuppose cultic devotion to Jesus as a familiar and defining feature of Christian circles wherever they were found (e.g., 1 Cor. 1:2). So, instead of an evolutionary/incremental model, we have to think in terms of something more adequate. What we have suggested in the evidence is a more explosively quick phenomenon, a religious development that was more like a volcanic eruption. . . . [I]t was a major and unprecedented move for people influenced by the exclusivist monotheistic stance of Second-Temple Judaism to include another figure singularly alongside God as recipient of cultic devotion in their worship gatherings. That is, in the devotional practices and attendant beliefs of earliest Christian circles, Jesus was linked with God in astonishing and unprecedented ways.[13]

Hurtado sees this worship of Christ reflected in the New Testament writings in the following six ways:

[11] Bradshaw, "God, Christ, and the Holy Spirit," 53.

[12] In addition to his essay, "The Binitarian Pattern of Earliest Christian Devotion and Early Doctrinal Development" (note 7 above), see also *Lord Jesus Christ: Devotion to Jesus in Earliest Christianity* (Grand Rapids, MI: Eerdmans, 2003), and *How on Earth Did Jesus Become a God? Historical Questions about Earliest Devotion to Jesus* (Grand Rapids, MI: Eerdmans, 2005).

[13] Hurtado, *How on Earth Did Jesus Become a God?*, 25.

(1) hymns about Jesus sung as part of early Christian worship; (2) prayer to God "through" Jesus and "in Jesus' name," and even direct prayer to Jesus himself, including particularly the invocation of Jesus in the corporate worship setting; (3) "calling upon the name of Jesus," particularly in Christian baptism and in healing and exorcism; (4) the Christian common meal enacted as a sacred meal where the risen Jesus presides as "Lord" of the gathered community; (5) the practice of ritually "confessing" Jesus in the context of Christian worship; and (6) Christian prophecy as oracles of the risen Jesus, and the Holy Spirit of prophecy understood as also the Spirit of Jesus.[14]

Of particular interest for this chapter is Hurtado's exegetical treatment of what has been called the "Christ Hymn" or "Christological Ode" of Philippians 2:5-11, a liturgical hymn sung in corporate worship, according to the view of most New Testament scholars.

Let the same mind be in you that was in Christ Jesus, who, though he was in the form of God, did not regard equality with God as something to be exploited, but emptied himself, taking the form of a slave, being born in human likeness. And being found in human form, he humbled himself and became obedient to the point of death—even death on a cross.

Therefore God also highly exalted him and gave him the name that is above every name, so that at the name of Jesus every knee should bend, in heaven and on earth and under the earth, and every tongue should confess that Jesus Christ is Lord, to the glory of God the Father.

While space does not permit a detailed presentation of his work, Hurtado's conclusions represent a significant shift in the way that modern biblical scholarship has come to interpret this text. That is, this ode reflects neither a Gnostic "redeemer-myth" nor a First Adam–Second Adam juxtaposition between disobedience and obedience, since, supposedly, both Adams were originally in the "form of God" (*morphē theou*), a phrase understood by other scholars as equivalent to "image of God" (*eikon theou*). Rather, Hurtado argues that this text, much like the later Johannine prologue (John 1:1-18) of the 80s or 90s, is precisely about Jesus' "preexistence" in the "form" (not

[14] Ibid., 28.

"image") of God and his kenosis in the incarnation and death on the cross and his exaltation to share in the very divine name of God (YHWH, *Kyrios* or Lord), at which every knee is to bow in worship.[15] If Hurtado's analysis is correct, even as early as the New Testament writings of the 50s and 60s the relationship between liturgical prayer and doctrine was already being established. In fact, Hurtado concludes elsewhere not only that there is a *relationship* between worship and doctrine but that it was the very worship pattern itself "in which Jesus was given a place that linked him with the one God in unparalleled ways" that became one of the "major driving forces" leading to a theological understanding of God and Christ. And the kind of theological understanding needed was one "that explained, justified, and measured up to the remarkable pattern of Christian binitarian worship/devotion."[16] Even in the earliest layers of Christianity, therefore, praying was shaping believing; worship was forming doctrine. The *lex orandi* was already constituting in some way the *lex credendi*.

Such an approach to the relationship between liturgical prayer and Christology is also demonstrable from other sources beyond the New Testament writings in the first three centuries. Not only do we have early evidence of direct address to Christ in the eucharistic prayers of the late first- and early second-century *Didache*, with the invocation "Marana tha" (Our Lord, come!), a liturgical invocation also present in the New Testament (1 Cor 16:22; Rev 22:20), but in approximately the same time period Ignatius of Antioch can appeal to the eucharistic liturgy against what he considers to be the heterodox christological position of the Docetists:

> They [Docetists] hold aloof from the Eucharist and from services of prayer, because they refuse to admit that the Eucharist is the flesh of our Saviour Jesus Christ, which suffered for our sins and which, in his goodness, the Father raised [from the dead].[17]

---

[15] Ibid., 83–107.

[16] Hurtado, "The Binitarian Pattern," 49–50.

[17] *Smyrnaeans* 6. Translated from Ignatius of Antioch, *Letters* (c. 115), LCC 1, trans. Cyril C. Richardson (Philadelphia: Westminster, 1953), 108–9. On Ignatius and the Eucharist, see Frederick Klawiter, "The Eucharist and Sacramental Realism in the Thought of St. Ignatius of Antioch," *Studia Liturgica* 37 (2007): 129–63.

In the eucharistic-type prayer, known as the Prayer of Polycarp, long thought to be second century in date but more recently dated in the middle of the third century,[18] the about-to-be-martyred bishop not only praises God *through* Christ, the "eternal and heavenly high Priest," but even at this early date ascribes equal glory *to* Christ and the Holy Spirit as well:

Lord God Almighty, Father of thy beloved and blessed Servant Jesus Christ, through whom we have received full knowledge of thee, "the God of angels and powers and all creation" and of the whole race of the righteous who live in thy presence: I bless thee, because thou hast deemed me worthy of this day and hour, to take my part in the number of the martyrs, in the cup of thy Christ, for "resurrection to eternal life" of soul and body in the immortality of the Holy Spirit; among whom may I be received in thy presence this day as a rich and acceptable sacrifice, just as thou hast prepared and revealed beforehand and fulfilled, thou that art the true God without any falsehood. For this and for everything I praise thee, I bless thee, I glorify thee, through the eternal and heavenly High Priest, Jesus Christ, thy beloved Servant, through whom be glory to thee with him and Holy Spirit both now and unto the ages to come. Amen.[19]

Other examples of prayer addressed to Christ, as well as to the Holy Spirit, come from the Syrian East in this early period. In those mid-third-century texts known as the Syrian *Acts of the Apostles*, sometimes called the "Apocryphal Acts," several descriptions of baptismal and eucharistic liturgies occur, reflecting the shape and contents of those rites in the third century. Of particular interest are the following eucharistic texts:

Acts of John, 85, 109: We glorify thy name that converteth us from error and pitiless deceit; we glorify thee who hast shown before our eyes what we have seen; we testify to thy goodness, in various ways appearing; we praise thy gracious name, O Lord, [which] has convicted those that are convicted by thee; we thank thee, Lord Jesus Christ, that we confide in [. . .], which is unchanging; we thank thee who hadst

---

[18] See Moss, *The Other Christs*, 196–97.

[19] *The Martyrdom of Polycarp* 18, in C. Richardson, *Early Christian Fathers*, LCC 1 (Philadelphia: Westminster, 1953), 154.

need [. . .] of [our] nature that is being saved; we thank thee that hast given us this unwavering [faith] that thou alone art [God] both now and for ever; we thy servants, that are assembled and gathered with [good] cause, give thanks to thee, O holy one.

What praise or what offering or what thanksgiving shall we name as we break this bread, but thee alone, Jesu. We glorify thy name of Father which was spoken by thee; we glorify thy name of Son which was spoken by thee. We glorify thine entering of the door; we glorify thy Resurrection that is shown us through thee; we glorify thy Way; we glorify thy Seed, the Word, Grace, Faith, the Salt, the inexpressible Pearl, the Treasure, the Plough; the Net, the Greatness, the Diadem, him that for our sakes was called the Son of Man, the truth, repose, knowledge, power, commandment, confidence, liberty and refuge in thee. For thou alone, O Lord, are the root of immortality and the fount of incorruption and the seat of the aeons, who art called all these things on our account, that calling on thee through them we may know thy greatness, which at the present is invisible to us, but visible only to the pure as it is portrayed in thy man only.[20]

Acts of Thomas, 49–50:[21] Jesus, who has made us worthy to partake of the Eucharist of thy holy body and blood, behold we make bold to approach thy Eucharist, and to call upon thy holy name; come thou and have fellowship with us! . . . [Come gift of the Most High;] Come, perfect compassion; Come fellowship of the male; [Come, Holy Spirit;] Come, thou that dost know the mysteries of the Chosen; Come, thou that hast part in all the combats of the noble Athlete; [Come, treasure of glory; Come, darling of the compassion of the Most High;] Come, silence that dost reveal the great deeds of the whole greatness; Come, thou that dost show forth the hidden things and make the ineffable manifest; Holy Dove that bearest the twin young; Come, hidden Mother; Come, thou that art manifest in thy deeds and dost furnish joy and rest for all that are joined with thee; Come and partake with us in this Eucharist which we celebrate in thy name, and in this love-feast [*agape*] in which we are gathered together at thy call.

[20] English translation from New Testament Apocrypha II, ed. W. Schneemelcher (Cambridge: James Clarke; Louisville: Westminster/John Knox Press, 1992), 200–202. On the dating of the Acts of John, see G. Winkler, "Nochmals zu den Anfängen der Epiklese und des Sanctus im Eucharistischen Hochgebet," *Theologisches Quartalschrift* 74, no. 3 (1994): 214–31.

[21] Translated from *New Testament Apocrypha* II, 359–60, 391–92, 401.

Acts of Thomas, 133: [Bread] of life, those who eat of which remain incorruptible; bread which fills hungry souls with its blessing—thou art the one [thought worthy] to receive a gift, that thou mayest become for us forgiveness of sins, and they who eat it become immortal. We name over thee the name of the mother of the ineffable mystery of the hidden dominions and powers, we name [over thee the name of Jesus]. . . . Let the power of blessing come and [settle upon the bread], that all the souls which partake of it may be washed of their sins!

Acts of Thomas, 158: Thy holy body which was crucified for us we eat, and thy blood which was poured out for us for salvation we drink. Let thy body, then, become for us salvation, and thy blood for remission of sins.

Based on these and other texts from the Syrian Acts, Gabriele Winkler,[22] together with earlier work by Sebastian Brock,[23] has argued that the origins of the baptismal and eucharistic epicleses (invocations) over the oil, water, bread, and wine are to be found in the direct address liturgical invocations like the biblical *Marana tha*, namely, "Come, Holy Spirit," or "Come, Name of the Messiah" (*Acts of Thomas*, 27), and others. Other types of liturgical epicleses addressed to the Father and requesting that he "let come" (an intermediate stage) or "send" the Holy Spirit belong to later euchological composition shaped by later trinitarian theology. To this we shall return below.[24]

One of the most well-known liturgical prayers from this Syrian tradition, of course, is the Anaphora of Addai and Mari, a prayer usually dated in the same third-century context as the Syrian *Acts of the Apostles* but known only from much later manuscripts, which contain most likely numerous additions.

Priest:	Peace be with you.
Answer:	And with you and your spirit.
Priest:	The grace of our Lord . . .
Answer: Amen.	

[22] See Winkler, "Nochmals zu den Anfängen," 217–20.

[23] S. Brock, "The Epiklesis in the Antiochene Baptismal *Ordines*," in *Symposium Syriacum 1972*, Oirentalia Christiana Analecta 197 (Rome: Pontificio Istituto Orientale, 1974), 183–218.

[24] See below, 43–44.

Priest: Up with your minds.

Answer: They are with you, O God.

Priest: The offering is offered to God, the Lord of all.

Answer: It is fitting and right.

The priest . . . : Worthy of glory from every mouth and thanksgiving from every tongue is the adorable and glorious name of the Father and of the Son and of the Holy Spirit. He created the world through his grace and its inhabitants in his compassion; he saved people through his mercy, and gave great grace to mortals.

Your majesty, O Lord, a thousand thousand heavenly beings adore; myriad myriads of angels, and ranks of spiritual beings, seraphim, glorify your name, crying out and glorifying . . . :

People: Holy, holy . . .

The priest . . . : And with these heavenly armies we, also, even we, your lowly, weak, and miserable servants, Lord, give you thanks because you have brought about us a great grace which cannot be repaid. For you put on our human nature to give us life through your divine nature; you raised us from our lowly state; you restored our Fall; you restored our immortality; you forgave our debts; you justified our sinfulness; you enlightened our intelligence. You, our Lord and our God, conquered our enemies, and made the lowliness of our weak nature to triumph through the abundant mercy of your grace. . . .

. . . You, Lord, through your many mercies which cannot be told, be graciously mindful of all the pious and righteous Fathers who were pleasing in your sight, in the commemoration of the body and blood of your Christ, which we offer to you on the pure and holy altar, as you taught us.

And grant us your tranquility and your peace for all the days of this age. . . . That all the inhabitants of the earth may know you, that you sent our Lord Jesus Christ, your beloved Son, and he, our Lord and our God, taught us through his life-giving gospel all the purity and holiness of the prophets, apostles, martyrs, confessors, bishops, priests, deacons, and all children of the holy Catholic Church who have been sealed with the living seal of holy baptism.

And we also, Lord, (*thrice*) your lowly, weak, and miserable servants, who have gathered and stand before you, [and] have received through tradition the form which is from you, rejoicing, exalting, commemorating, and celebrating this mystery of the passion, death and resurrection of our Lord Jesus Christ.

May your Holy Spirit, Lord, come and rest on this offering of your servants, and bless and sanctify it, that it may be to us, Lord, for remission of debts, forgiveness of sins, and the great hope of resurrection from the dead, and new life in the kingdom of heaven, with all who have been pleasing in your sight.

And because of all your wonderful dispensation towards us, with open mouths and uncovered faces we give you thanks and glorify you without ceasing in your Church, which has been redeemed by the precious blood of your Christ.[25]

This eucharistic prayer in a form very much like the text above is still used today both by the Ancient Church of the East and by East Syrian Catholics (the Assyro-Chaldean and the Syro-Malabar Churches) and has a close relationship to one also still used by the Maronites called the Anaphora of St. Peter (or *Sharar* from its first word in Syriac).[26] In our recent book on the Eucharist, Paul Bradshaw and I offer a very tentative reconstruction of what its most primitive version might have been:

Glory to you, the adorable and glorious Name, who created the world in his grace and its inhabitants in his compassion, and redeemed humankind in his mercy, and has wrought great grace towards mortals.

We, Lord, your sinful servants, give you thanks because you have brought about in us your grace that cannot be repaid; you put on our humanity to give us life through your divinity; you lifted up our low state and raised our fall; you restored our immortality; you forgave our debts, you justified our sinfulness, you enlightened our understanding, you vanquished our enemies and made triumphant our

[25] Translation from PEER, 42–44.
[26] For an English translation of *Sharar*, see ibid., 46–50.

lowliness. For all your graces towards us, we send up to you glory
and honor, now and for ever and ever.

Lord, in your abundant mercies make a gracious remembrance
of all the upright and just fathers, of the prophets, apostles, martyrs
and confessors. . . .

And for your wonderful plan for us, we, redeemed by your blood
give you thanks with open mouth in your church, now and for ever
and ever.[27]

Attention is often given to this anaphora because its earliest version, like the *Didache*, does not contain the narrative of Christ's institution of the Eucharist from the Synoptic or Pauline accounts of
the Last Supper. And it is a version without that narrative that is still
prayed regularly today in the Ancient Church of the East.[28] But what
is equally significant is that, while the beginning of the current form
of the prayer acknowledges the "Name" of the Holy Trinity and lists
Father, Son, and Holy Spirit, the language of the prayer following the
Sanctus shifts between addressing Christ and/or the Father directly.
Although several scholars[29] have tried to explain this as reflecting the
early trinitarian heresy called Modalistic Monarchianism or Sabellian-
ism, which made no personal distinctions between Father, Son, and
Holy Spirit as each "Person" was but a temporary mask put on by the
one God,[30] other scholars, most notably Bryan Spinks,[31] following an

[27] Paul F. Bradshaw and Maxwell E. Johnson, *The Eucharistic Liturgies: Their Evolution and Interpretation* (Collegeville, MN: Liturgical Press, Pueblo, 2012), 40. Translation adapted from Sarhad Jammo, "The Anaphora of the Apostles Addai and Mari: A Study of Structure and Background," *Orientalia Christiana Periodica* 68 (2002): 5–35, although not accepting his reconstruction in all respects.

[28] See Nicholas Russo, "The Validity of the Anaphora of *Addai and Mari*: Cri-
tique of the Critiques," in *Issues in Eucharistic Praying in East and West: Essays in Liturgical and Theological Analysis*, ed. Maxwell E. Johnson (Collegeville, MN: Liturgical Press, Pueblo, 2010), 21–62.

[29] Cf. Anthony Gelston, *The Eucharistic Prayer of Addai and Mari* (Oxford: Clarendon Press, 1992); and S. Jammo, "The Anaphora of the Apostles Addai and Mari."

[30] On Monarchianism and Sebellianism, see Jaroslav Pelikan, *The Christian Tra-
dition: A History of the Development of Doctrine*, vol.1: *The Emergence of the Catholic Tradition (100–600)* (Chicago: University of Chicago Press, 1971), 175ff.

[31] Spinks, "The Place of Christ," 10–12; idem, *Addai and Mari—The Anaphora of the Apostles: A Text for Students*, Grove Liturgical Study 24 (Bramcote: Grove Books,

earlier hypothesis of E. C. Ratcliff[32] and, to some extent, of William
Macomber,[33] have contended that the earliest version of the prayer
would most likely have been addressed all the way through to Christ
alone, as in our reconstruction above. Such a position, they believe, is
actually supported by the Maronite *Sharar*, which is directed to Christ
exclusively from the *Sanctus* to the end of the prayer and, hence,
does not oscillate between addressing Christ or the Father as does
Addai and Mari in its current form. Even later eucharistic prayers
containing sections addressed directly to Christ, and often discarded
by Jungmann as Monophysite in theology, such as the Syriac version
of the Anaphora of St. James (the eucharistic prayer most associated
with Jerusalem liturgy) or the Egyptian Anaphora of St. Gregory
of Nazianzus, may well be preserving this earlier tradition in their
formulation.[34]

If the Syrian East is particularly rich in examples of liturgical and
other prayers addressed directly to Christ, such practices also appear
in the Greek-speaking churches, although they are less abundant. We
have already seen that Origen of Alexandria is credited with the so-
called classic form of Christian prayer being addressed *to* the Father
through the Son *in* the Holy Spirit, a structure, as will be seen below,
that *does* play a role in the debates surrounding the dispute over the
divinity of the Holy Spirit. But, as Paul Bradshaw has shown most
recently,[35] this is not the only prayer structure known to or advocated
by him. Rather, Origen himself is actually an advocate both of prayer
to the saints, as we shall see in the next chapter, and of direct prayer
made to Christ. As evidence of this, Bradshaw directs our attention
to the following two passages from Origen's *Contra Celsum*:[36]

1980); and idem, "The Original Form of the Anaphora of the Apostles Addai and
Mari," in idem, *Worship: Prayers from the East* (Washington, DC: Pastoral Press,
1993), 21–36, here at 29–34.

[32] Edward Craddock Ratcliff, "The Original Form of the Anaphora of *Addai and
Mari*: A Suggestion," *Journal of Theological Studies* 30 (1928–29): 23–32.

[33] William Macomber, "The Oldest Known Text of the Anaphora of the Apostles
Addai and Mari," *Orientalia Christiana Periodica* 32 (1966): 335–71.

[34] See Spinks, "The Place of Christ," 12.

[35] Bradshaw, "God, Christ, and the Holy Spirit," 58.

[36] Translations as cited by ibid. are taken from *Contra Celsum*, trans. Henry
Chadwick (Cambridge: Cambridge University Press, 1953).

Contra Celsum 5.4: We have to send up every petition, prayer, intercession, and thanksgiving to the supreme God through the high-priest of all angels, the living and divine Logos. We will even make our petitions to the very Logos himself and offer intercessions to him and give thanks and also pray to him.

Contra Celsum 8.26: [W]e ought to pray to the supreme God alone, and to pray besides to the only begotten Logos of God, the firstborn of all creation; and we ought to beseech him, as a high-priest, to bear our prayer, when it has reached him, up to his God and our God and to his Father and the Father of people who live according to the word of God.

Origen's above references to prayer being offered directly to the divine Logos is significant for another reason liturgically. That is, there is also a tradition within the Greek-speaking churches, including the writings of Origen, which associates the "consecration" of the eucharistic bread and cup directly to the activity of the Logos. This comes to its best-known expression as a specific consecratory "Logos-epiclesis" in the mid-fourth-century eucharistic prayer (Prayer 1) and in the prayer for the blessing of the baptismal waters (Prayer 7) in the Egyptian *Euchologion* or collection of prayers of Bishop Sarapion of Thmuis:[37]

Prayer 1: God of truth, let your holy Word (Logos) come upon this bread in order that the bread may become body of the Word, and upon this cup in order that the cup may become blood of truth. And make all those who partake to receive a medicine of life for the healing of every illness, and for the strengthening of every advancement and virtue, not for condemnation, God of truth, not for testing and reproach.

Prayer 7: Look now from heaven and gaze upon these waters and fill them with Holy Spirit. Let your inexpressible word (Logos) come to be in them. Let it change their operation and make them generative, being filled with your grace, so that the mystery now being

[37] On Sarapion of Thmuis, see Maxwell E. Johnson, *The Prayers of Sarapion of Thmuis: A Liturgical, Literary, and Theological Analysis*, Orientalia Christiana Analecta 249 (Rome: Pontificio Istituto Orientale, 1995). English translation of the prayers is taken from this study.

accomplished may not be found empty in those being born again, but
may fill with divine grace all those who go down and are baptized.
. . . And as your only-begotten word (Logos), when he descended
upon the waters of the Jordan made them holy, so also now let him
descend into these. Let him make them holy and spiritual in order
that those who are baptized may no longer be flesh and blood but
spiritual and able to give worship to you.

While some scholars in the past, most notably Bernard Botte,[38] ques-
tioned the orthodoxy of these epicleses and saw them as reflecting a
deliberate and heretical attempt to downplay the divinity of the Holy
Spirit in a post-Nicene context, recent scholarship has defended both
the orthodoxy and antiquity of these prayers. In so doing, scholars
point to texts by Justin Martyr, Irenaeus of Lyons, and Origen that
underscore the activity of the Logos, especially in the Eucharist. We
shall look at each of these authors briefly.

In his *First Apology*, written to the Roman emperor Antoninus Pius,
Justin Martyr (d. 165) provides the following interpretation of the
"food" of the Eucharist:

> *Apology* 1.66.2: Just as, through the word of God, our Savior Jesus
> Christ became Incarnate and took upon Himself flesh and blood for
> our salvation, so, we have been taught, the food which has been made
> the Eucharist by the prayer of His word (δι' εὐχῆς λόγου τοῦ παρ' αὐτοῦ),
> and which nourishes our flesh and blood by assimilation, is both the
> flesh and blood of that Jesus who was made flesh.[39]

It is, of course, difficult to know with certainty what Justin intends by
the phrase δι' εὐχῆς λόγου in this text. While Geoffrey Cuming argued
that he is referring to a formula or "form of words" through Jesus
(i.e., the institution narrative),[40] Anthony Gelston claims that the best
interpretation is that Justin's words are to be taken as a reference to
the whole eucharistic prayer itself. In other words, it is not a prayer

---

[38] B. Botte, "L'Euchologe de Sérapion, est-il authentique?," *Oriens Christianus*
48 (1964): 50–56.

[39] Translation from ANF 1, 185.

[40] Geoffrey Cuming, "DI' EUCHES LOGOU (Justin Apology 1.66.2)," *Journal
of Theological Studies* 31 (1980): 80-82.

formula ("form of words") but prayer itself (a "word of prayer") that Justin intends by this phrase.[41] S. Agrelo argues in a manner similar to that of Gelston and concludes that just as Justin understands the Logos to be the agent of his own incarnation, so also is the Logos to be understood as the one who brings about his own flesh and blood in the Eucharist. In both cases, it is the reality of the flesh and blood of Christ that is the end result of the activity of the Logos. Consequently, it is the prayer of the presider that is the "prayer of the Logos," and the Logos "has as its main objective the reality of the body and blood and Christ."[42] A similar conclusion has been reached recently by Michael Heintz.[43]

An approach somewhat parallel to that of Justin is offered by Irenaeus of Lyons in his famous treatise, *Adversus Haereses* (*Against Heresies*):

> *Adversus Haereses* 4.18.5: When, therefore, the mingled cup and the manufactured bread receives the Word of God (ἐπιδέχεται τὸν λόγον του θεοῦ) . . . the Eucharist becomes the body and blood of Christ. . . . For as bread from the earth, receiving the invocation of God (προσλαβόμενος τὴν ἐπίκλησιν τοῦ θεοῦ) is no longer common bread but a Eucharist composed of two things, both an earthly and a heavenly one, so also our bodies, partaking of the Eucharist, are no longer corruptible, having the hope of eternal resurrection.[44]

Again, as in Justin, there is no clear indication that "the invocation of God" or "Word of God" refers either to an institution narrative or to an explicit anaphoral epiclesis of the Logos. Nevertheless, what is established is a parallel between the prayer of the church (the invocation or epiclesis of God) and the bread and cup's reception of the Logos of God. As Agrelo writes:

[41] A. Gelston, "DI' EUCHES LOGOU," *Journal of Theological Studies* 33 (1982): 172–75.

[42] S. Agrelo, "El 'Logos' divina que hace la eucaristia: Testimonio de san Justino," *Antonianum* 60 (1985): 601–63.

[43] Michael Heintz, "δι' εὐχῆς λόγου του παρ' αὐτοῦ (Justin, *Apology* I.66.2)," *Studia Liturgica* 33 (2003): 33–36.

[44] Translation from ANF 1, 486. A similar parallel is made by Irenaeus in *Adversus Haereses* 5.2.3 (ANF 1, 528).

The presence of the Lord's body and blood in the eucharist . . . is not independent of the elements of bread and wine, from which they have been formed; the operative presence of the Word of God in the celebration cannot be considered as independent of the word of the church which seeks it.[45]

Accordingly, the Logos is the operative agent who, in response to the church's invocation, "consecrates" the Eucharist as the Body and Blood of Christ.

Several texts from Origen, as noted above, also appear to make a similar connection between the Logos and the bread and cup of the Eucharist.

> *Com. in Matt.* 11.14: And in the case of the bread of the Lord, accordingly, there is advantage to him who uses it, when with undefiled mind and pure conscience he partakes of the bread. And so neither by not eating, I mean by the very fact that we do not eat of the bread, which has been sanctified by the word of God and prayer (τοῦ ἁλιασθέτος λόλῳ θεοῦ καὶ ἐντεύξει), are we deprived of any good thing; . . . but in respect of the prayer which comes upon it, according to the proportion of the faith, becomes a benefit and is a means of clear vision to the mind which looks to that which is beneficial, and it is not the material of the bread but the word which is said over it is of advantage to him who eats it not unworthily of the Lord.[46]
>
> *Contra Celsum* 8.33: We give thanks to the Creator of all, and, along with thanksgiving and prayer (μετ᾿ εὐχαριστίας καὶ εὐχῆς᾿) for the blessings we have received, we also eat the bread presented to us; and this bread becomes by prayer a sacred body, which sanctifies those who sincerely partake of it.[47]
>
> *In Matth. ser.* 85: That bread which God the Word (*deus verbum*) owns to be His Body, is the Word which nourishes the soul, the Word which proceeds from God the Word (*verbum de deo verbum procedens*), and that bread from heavenly bread which is placed upon the table. . . . And that drink which saturates and inebriates the hearts of those that drink it, the drink in that cup, of which it is said: How goodly is

---

[45] S. Agrelo, "Epíclesis y eucharistia en. S. Ireneo," *Ecclesia Orans* 3 (1986): 7–27, here at 26–27.

[46] Translation from ANF 10, 443.

[47] Translation from ANF 4, 651–52.

thy inebriating chalice (Ps. 22). . . . Not that visible bread which He held in His hands, did the Divine Logos call His body, but the word, in the mystery of which the bread was to be broken. Not that visible drink did He call His blood, but the word, in the mystery of which this drink was to be poured out. For the body of the Divine Logos or His blood, what else can they be than the word which nourishes and the word which gladdens the hearts?[48]

That an explicit epiclesis of the Logos was known in the eucharistic liturgies of these various ante-Nicene theologians remains to be proven. Edward Kilmartin notes, however, that prior to the middle of the fourth century:

the uniqueness of Jesus is explained by a Logos Christology or a Spirit Christology. But the limits of the latter christology, at an earlier date, must be recognized. Justin Martyr speaks of the Logos effecting his own incarnation, identifying the Spirit of Luke 1:35 with the Logos. From the middle of the second to the middle of the fourth century, the Logos is frequently described as providing the essential anointing of his humanity by the assumption itself. But in the latter part of the fourth century, in the wake of the controversies over the divinity of the Holy Spirit, more attention is paid to the role of the Spirit in the conception of Jesus. . . . Up to the middle of the fourth century the Logos, generally viewed as accomplishing his own incarnation, was also understood as the one who effects the change of bread and wine into his body and blood. Afterwards, the Holy Spirit is assigned both the role of effecting the incarnation and the transformation of the Eucharistic gifts in Greek theology.[49]

And, on the basis of some of the patristic sources cited above, Johannes Betz similarly concluded with reference to the explicit Logos-epiclesis in the prayers of Sarapion of Thmuis that:

the special *Logos-epiclesis* is already well attested for Egypt in Clement, Origen, Athanasius. It must therefore be treated in Sarapion as a

---

[48] Translation from P. Jacquemont, "Origen," in *The Eucharist of the Early Christians*, ed. Willy Rordorf et al. (New York: Pueblo, 1978), 187–88.

[49] Edward Kilmartin, *Christian Liturgy: Theology and Practice*, vol. 1: *Systematic Theology* (Kansas City: Sheed & Ward, 1988), 165–66.

primitive formula, not as a correction. If the Prayers of Sarapion do not yet have a fully developed doctrinal precision regarding Logos and Pneuma, that is no valid argument against their authenticity.[50]

There can be little doubt that the Logos-epicleses we see in the prayers of Sarapion of Thmuis are consistent theologically with these earlier sources, although we cannot conclude with certainty that an explicit invocation of the Logos was known by these particular authors. Yet, even in Origen's use of "body of the Divine Logos," for example, is there a eucharistic parallel with Sarapion's phrase requesting that the bread might become the very "body of the Logos."

Furthermore, there does appear to be a kind of parallel established here with those early Syrian invocations directly addressing the Holy Spirit and/or Name of the Messiah to "come," and it certainly cannot be ruled out that Sarapion's Logos-epiclesis is but a later stage in the development of similar invocations in the early Greek-speaking communities. As noted above, in his study of the epiclesis in Antiochene baptismal *ordines*, Sebastian Brock, followed by Winkler, convincingly argues for the antiquity of the verb "come" and the later introduction of the verb "send" in relation to the invocation of the Holy Spirit on the baptismal waters in this Syriac-speaking tradition.[51] In addition, Brock notes that the earliest stage in this Syrian development addressed the epiclesis directly to Christ and requested that he himself "come." A second stage, according to him, asks Christ that "his Spirit may come," and in the final stage, before fifth-century Greek influence brought about the use of "send," God was asked that the Spirit "may come."[52]

---

[50] Johannes Betz, *Eucharistie: in der Schrift und Patristik* (Basil and Vienna, 1979), 65n8, as cited by Geoffrey Cuming, *The Liturgy of St. Mark*, Orientalia Christiana Analecta 234 (Rome: Pontificio Istituto Orientale, 1990), xxxvii.

[51] Brock, "The Epiklesis," 183–215. For more recent work on the anaphoral epiclesis, see Anne McGowan, "The Epiclesis in Eucharistic Praying Reconsidered: Early Evidence and Recent Western Reforms," in *A Living Tradition: On the Intersection of Liturgical History and Pastoral Practice; Essays in Honor of Maxwell E. Johnson,* ed. David Pitt, Stefanos Alexopoulos, and Christian McConnell (Collegeville, MN: Liturgical Press, Pueblo, 2012), 230–55.

[52] Brock, "The Epiklesis," 213–14.

Although the first part of Sarapion's prayer for the "Sanctification of Waters" (Prayer 7) asks that God might "look" from heaven, "gaze upon," and "fill" the baptismal waters with the Holy Spirit, neither prayer contains the verb "send" in relation to either the Holy Spirit or the Logos. Rather, in their invocations of the Logos, both of them use some form of "come": either γενέσθω or καταρχέσθω as in Prayer 7 or ἐπιδημησάτω as in the anaphora (Prayer 1). If Brock's analysis of the development of epicletic verbs in the Syrian baptismal tradition is correct, something quite similar may have taken place also within the Egyptian tradition. Here, in fact, is a parallel to the intermediate stage of "let come," though, as Winkler has noted, "rest" or "abide" in the eucharistic gifts may be a more accurate translation of ἐπιδημησάτω than either "come upon" or "let come."[53] But this might actually make some kind of "Syrian connection" stronger. As I have pointed out elsewhere,[54] in the Greek version of the prayer for the consecration of the prebaptismal oil in *Acts of Thomas* 157, the following text appears:

> Jesus . . . let the power come and be established in this oil . . .
> let the gift also come . . . and let it rest upon [ἐπιδημῆσαι] this oil,
> whereupon we invoke your holy name.[55]

Here in this translated Syrian text is the same verb that appears in the anaphora of Sarapion in conjunction with the epiclesis of the Logos. It may still be, then, that in spite of the absence of the term Logos in the early Syrian liturgical sources, Sarapion's epicleses of the Logos might well represent an early stage in the development of the Egyptian epiclesis within a world of thought so conceptually and theologically distinct, a stage which preserves both an archaic verb form and an archaic theology of the role of the Logos in the liturgical-sacramental rites of the church.

[53] Winkler, "Nochmals zu den Anfängen," 218–19.

[54] "The Origins of the Anaphoral Use of the Sanctus and Epiclesis Revisited: The Contribution of Gabriele Winkler and Its Implications," in *Crossroad of Cultures: Studies in Liturgy and Patristics in Honor of Gabriele Winkler*, ed. H-J. Feulner, E. Velkovska, and R. Taft, Orientalia Christiana Analecta 260 (Rome: Pontifical Oriental Institute, 2000), 438–40.

[55] Greek text as cited by Winkler, "Weitere Beobachtungen zur frühen Epiklese (den Doxologien und dem Sanctus). Über die Bedeutung der Apokryphen für die Erforschung der Entwicklung der Riten," *Oriens Christianus* 80 (1996): 191.

Two fourth-century christological hymns, or hymns with strong christological content and direct address to Christ, should be noted here as well: first, the *Gloria in Excelsis*, which originated in the Greek-speaking East and is sung traditionally at *Orthros* (Matins) and, of course, later within the opening rites of the eucharistic liturgy in the West; and second, the Western *Te Deum*, still sung in the West at Vigils, Nocturns, or Matins (now the "Office of Readings") on Sundays and major feasts. The christological portion of the *Gloria in Excelsis* constitutes the second section of this hymn, with the first addressed to God the Father:

> Lord Jesus Christ, Only Begotten Son,
> Lord God, Lamb of God, Son of the Father,
> you take away the sins of the world,
>   have mercy on us;
> you take away the sins of the world,
>   receive our prayer;
> you are seated at the right hand of the Father,
>   have mercy on us.
> For you alone are the Holy One,
> you alone are the Lord,
> you alone are the Most High,
> Jesus Christ,
> with the Holy Spirit,
> in the glory of God the Father.
> Amen.[56]

Because book 7.47 of the late fourth-century *Apostolic Constitutions* contains a version of this hymn wherein the christological section is turned into an address to the Father,[57] some have wanted to argue that the christological address is a later development and hence supportive of a more primitive form of prayer *through* Christ. Thanks to the work of J. Lebreton and others, however, the current scholarly view is that the address to Christ is original.[58]

---

[56] *The Roman Missal, Third Edition* (Collegeville, MN: Liturgical Press, 2011).

[57] *Lex Constitutions apostoliques* III, SC 336, ed. Marcel Metzger (Paris: Éditions du Cerf, 1987), 112–13.

[58] See J. Lebreton, "La forme primitive du *Gloria in excelsis*, prière au Christ, ou priere à Dieu le Pére?," *Recherche de science religieuse* 13 (1923): 322–29. See also

Like the *Gloria*, the *Te deum* is also composed with the first section addressed to God the Father, even including a version of the *Sanctus*, with the second major section addressed to Christ:

> O Christ, the King of glory!
>> You alone are the Father's eternal Son.
> When you became man so as to save humankind,
>> you did not shrink back from the chaste virgin's womb.
> When you triumphantly destroyed death's sting,
>> you opened up to believers the kingdom of heaven.
> You are now enthroned at God's right hand, in the Father's glory.
>> We believe that you will come for judgment.
> We therefore implore you to grant your servants grace and aid,
>> for you shed your precious blood for their redemption.
> Admit them all to the ranks of your saints
>> in everlasting glory.
> Be the Savior of your faithful people, Lord;
>> grant them your blessing, for they belong to you.
> Be their Shepherd, Lord,
>> uphold and exalt them forever and ever.[59]

Although regularly dated in the fourth century, and often attributed to Nicetas of Remisiana (335–415, modern-day Serbia), if not Augustine or Ambrose themselves, E. Kähler viewed this "hymn" as constituting the preface, *Sanctus*, and post-*Sanctus* sections of a primitive eucharistic prayer, perhaps of third-century North African origin, but certainly before the middle of the fourth century.[60] Together with the *Gloria*, then, this text may also provide additional cumulative evidence for liturgical prayer to Christ before the Council of Nicea itself.

What, therefore, is the relationship between all of these texts we have looked at so far and the Nicene *homoousios*? On the one hand, that relationship is extremely difficult to determine for the simple reason that the worship of Christ as God or a god, as we have seen,

---

Marcel Metzger, "La theologies des Constitutions apostoliques par Clement," *Revue des sciences et religieuses* 57 (1983): 29–49, 112–22, 169–94, 273–94.

[59] Translation from *Benedictine Daily Prayer*, ed. Maxwell E. Johnson (Collegeville, MN: Liturgical Press, 2005), 907.

[60] E. Kähler, *Studien zum Te Deum und zur Geschichte des 24. Psalms in der Alten Kirche* (Göttingen: Vandenhoeck und Ruprecht, 1958).

certainly predates the Council of Nicea by several hundred years. And, for that matter, such worship is not dependent on the explicit doctrinal formulation of the relationship between Christ and the Father as articulated by the Nicene *homoousios*, and no one, to my knowledge, made any kind of reference to the worship of Christ as a source for adopting this particular expression at the Council of Nicea. Rather, even if Christ is understood theologically as an angel, a *deuteros theos* (a second or even secondary god), the "first" of God's creatures, the created Logos through whom God created and redeemed the world, approaches associated with Arius and his followers, the worship of Christ with the Father was certainly a given. Some scholars occasionally point to liturgical prayers presumably reflecting an Arian bias, such as the description of Christ as God's "notable worshiper" in the anaphora of book 8 of the late fourth-century Antiochene *Apostolic Constitutions*,[61] or Botte's critique of the Logos-epiclesis in the Prayers of Sarapion of Thmuis,[62] and we know of the popularity of "Arian hymnody" later in Constantinople and Milan, countered by orthodox nocturnal stational processions and hymns initiated by Chrysostom[63] and the composition of orthodox Office hymns by Ambrose, which ultimately were to have their effect on Augustine's own famous conversion.[64] But, generally speaking, the liturgies celebrated by both Arians and Orthodox alike were simply part of the developing rites coming to be associated with the particular patriarchal sees to which they belonged (in the East, Antioch and Alexandria; in the West, primarily Rome but also Milan). As we shall see in the next section, the issue is the interpretation of common liturgical forms, not different ones.

[61] For the text of this anaphora in English, see PEER, 104–13. For comments on the "Arianizing" theology of the redactor of the anaphora, see Metzger, "La theologies des Constitutions apostoliques par Clement," 29–49, 112–22, 169–94, 273–94.

[62] Botte, "L'Euchologe de Sérapion, est-il authentique?," 50–56.

[63] See John Baldovin, *The Urban Character of Christian Worship: The Origins, Development, and Meaning of Stational Liturgy*, Orientalia Christiana Analecta 228 (Rome: Pontificio Istituto Orientale, 1987), 183–85; and Robert F. Taft, *The Byzantine Rite: A Short History*, American Essays in Liturgy (Collegeville, MN: Liturgical Press, 1992), 30–33.

[64] See Augustine, *Confessions* 9.12 and 10.33.

On the other hand, the defenders of the Nicene *homoousios* perceived correctly that one of the issues at stake in this controversy was precisely the question of true or false worship of Christ. That is, if Christ were somehow the Logos created by God; or were a mixture of divinity and humanity, i.e., a *tertium quid*, a third thing altogether; or were but an angel; or were merely *homoiousios* (of similar or like essence) to the Father, then any worship of Christ would ultimately be the worship of a creature and so would constitute idolatry on the part of the worshiper. But Christ, says Nicea, is "begotten not created [not a 'creature'], of the same essence [reality] as the Father [*homoousion to patri*]." And because of this the question of true worship emerges as a crucial topic in the battle against Arianism. As Jaroslav Pelikan, one of those unique historians of dogma who took the formative role of liturgy seriously, writes:

> Whether angel or Son of God, the Arian Logos, though subordinate to the Father and not of the same ousia with him, was nevertheless worthy of worship. The Arians shared with other Christians the usage of paying to the Son of God an adoration that by right belonged to God alone. . . . The Arians found prayer to the Logos an unavoidable element of Christian worship. Yet by this inconsistency between their dogmatic principle and their liturgical practice the Arians were saying, in effect: "Abandon the worship of the creation, and then draw near and worship a creature and a work" [Athanasius, *Against the Arians* 1.8]. From the attacks of orthodox writers like Ambrose it is clear that the Arians refused to abandon the practice of worshiping Christ.[65]

And, further:

> By the homoousios . . . the expositors of Nicene doctrine attempted to safeguard the soteriological and liturgical concerns of the church, for which it was mandatory that Christ be divine. . . . Writing before Nicea, Athanasius . . . denounced paganism for "serving the creature rather than the Creator" and then for refusing to "worship the Logos, our Lord Jesus Christ the Savior." After Nicea, when he was involved in the Arian controversy, he made use of this contrast to argue that the worship of Christ by men and angels proved his

---

[65] Pelikan, *The Christian Tradition*, vol. 1, 198–99.

essential difference from all creatures, including angels; only if he was not a creature, but true God by nature, could worship be proper. . . . [For the Arians] their theological position and their liturgical practice were irreconcilable.[66]

In this Nicene and immediate post-Nicene context, then, the liturgical, christological, and soteriological come together into a brilliant orthodox doctrinal synthesis. In terms of Christology and soteriology, especially as expressed in the theology of Athanasius, if Christ is but a creature of God, then he cannot save humanity because he too would be in need of salvation himself. This approach is well summarized in Athanasius' famous phrase that in Christ's incarnation "God became what we are so that we could be made [Θεοποιηθῶμεν] what He is."[67] And, liturgically, essentially the same argument is advanced, namely, that if Christ is but a creature of God, even the first created, even a second(ary) God, then to worship him is idolatry. What's at stake here, liturgically, therefore, is the role of liturgical prayer not only in shaping but also in supporting and defending orthodox doctrine. And, as Spinks notes, following Balthasar Fisher, "sound liturgical piety absolutely depends on both the *per Christum* (*through* Christ) and the *ad Christum* (*to* Christ)."[68]

2. Baptism, Doxology, and the Divinity of the Holy Spirit

If the question of true and false worship of Christ played a significant role in the development and defense of the Nicene *homoousios*, the language of worship itself, via the Greek verbs προσκυνέω (*proskuneo*, literally, to "worship" or to "fall down and worship") and συνδοξάζω (*syndoxazo*, to "glorify together"), entered into the creedal formula about the divinity of the Holy Spirit adopted at the Council of Constantinople in 381 CE.

---

[66] Ibid., 206–7. See also Jaroslav Pelikan, *Credo: Historical and Theological Guide to Creeds and Confessions of Faith in the Christian Tradition* (New Haven: Yale University Press, 2003), 166ff.

[67] Athanasius, *De Incarnatione Verbi Dei*, 54.

[68] Spinks, "The Place of Christ," 19.

And in the Holy Spirit,
the Lord and life-giver,
Who proceeds from the Father,
Who is worshiped (*proskynoumenon*) and glorified (*syndoxazomenon*)
  together
With the Father and the Son,
Who spoke through the Prophets.[69]

Behind the adoption of this type of creedal language, of course, are debates between Orthodox theologians and those who became known as semi-Arians or *Pneumatomachoi* (enemies of the Spirit), sometimes called *Tropikoi* because they appeared to Athanasius and others to be "moody" with regard to the identity of the Holy Spirit. And what is important to note is that within these debates appeal is made to the activity of the Holy Spirit not only in doing divine works in general (e.g., sanctification, inspiration of the prophets, miracles, and the resurrection of the dead) but, as we shall see, for our purposes in this chapter, specifically to the work of the Spirit in baptism and to the Spirit being addressed by liturgical praise and doxology.

The first author who refers clearly to baptism in his post-Nicene defense of the divinity of the Holy Spirit against the semi-Arians is Athanasius of Alexandria. In Discourses 2 and 4 of his famous *Contra Arianos*, or *Four Discourses against the Arians*,[70] he makes appeal to what appears to be the formula of baptism "in the name of the Father, and of the Son, and of the Holy Spirit," as indicative of the united saving activity of the trinitarian God:

> 2.41. But let the other heresies and the Manichees also know that the Father of the Christ is One, and is Lord and Maker of the creation through His proper Word. And let the Ariomaniacs know in particular, that the Word of God is One, being the only Son proper and genuine from His Essence, and having with His Father the oneness of Godhead indivisible, as we said many times, being taught it by the Saviour Himself. Since, were it not so, wherefore through Him

[69] *Creeds of the Churches: A Reader in Christian Doctrine from the Bible to the Present*, trans. John H. Leith, 3rd ed. (Louisville, KY: Westminster/John Knox Press, 1982), 33.
[70] NPNF, 4, 2nd series, pp. 370–71; 441.

does the Father create, and in Him reveal Himself to whom He will, and illuminate them? Or why too in the baptismal consecration is the Son named together with the Father? For if they say that the Father is not all-sufficient, then their answer is irreligious, but if He be, for this it is right to say, what is the need of the Son for framing the worlds, or for the holy laver? For what fellowship is there between creature and Creator? Or why is a thing made classed with the Maker in the consecration of all of us? Or why, as you hold, is faith in one Creator and in one creature delivered to us? For if it was that we might be joined to the Godhead, what need of the creature? But if that we might be united to the Son a creature, superfluous, according to you, is this naming of the Son in Baptism, for God who made Him a Son is able to make us sons also. Besides, if the Son be a creature, the nature of rational creatures being one, no help will come to creatures from a creature, since all need grace from God. We said a few words just now on the fitness that all things should be made by Him; but since the course of the discussion has led us also to mention holy Baptism, it is necessary to state, as I think and believe, that the Son is named with the Father, not as if the Father were not all-sufficient, not without meaning, and by accident; but, since He is God's Word and own Wisdom, and being His Radiance, is ever with the Father, therefore it is impossible, if the Father bestows grace, that He should not give it in the Son, for the Son is in the Father as the radiance in the light. For, not as if in need, but as a Father in His own Wisdom hath God rounded the earth, and made all things in the Word which is from Him, and in the Son confirms the Holy Laver. For where the Father is, there is the Son, and where the light, there the radiance; and as what the Father worketh, He worketh through the Son, and the Lord Himself says, "What I see the Father do, that do I also"; so also when baptism is given, whom the Father baptizes, him the Son baptizes; and whom the Son baptizes, he is consecrated in the Holy Ghost. And again as when the sun shines, one might say that the radiance illuminates, for the light is one and indivisible, nor can be detached, so where the Father is or is named, there plainly is the Son also; and is the Father named in Baptism? Then must the Son be named with Him.

2.42. . . . And these too hazard the fulness of the mystery, I mean Baptism; for if the consecration is given to us into the Name of Father and Son, and they do not confess a true Father, because they deny what is from Him and like His Essence, and deny also the true Son, and name another of their own framing as created out of nothing, is not the rite administered by them altogether empty and unprofitable, making a show, but in reality being no help towards religion? For the Arians do not baptize into Father and Son, but into Creator and creature, and into Maker and work. And as a creature is other than the Son, so the Baptism, which is supposed to be given by them, is other than the truth, though they pretend to name the Name of the Father and the Son, because of the words of Scripture, for not he who simply says, "O Lord," gives Baptism; but he who with the Name has also the right faith. On this account therefore our Saviour also did not simply command to baptize, but first says, "Teach"; then thus: "Baptize into the Name of Father, and Son, and Holy Ghost"; that the right faith might follow upon learning, and together with faith might come the consecration of Baptism.

4.21. And what more does the Word contribute to our salvation than the Son, if, as they hold, the Son is one, and the Word another? For the command is that we should believe, not in the Word, but in the Son. For John says, "He that believeth on the Son, hath everlasting life; but he that believeth not the Son, shall not see life." And Holy Baptism, in which the substance of the whole faith is lodged, is administered not in the Word, but in Father, Son, and Holy Ghost. If then, as they hold, the Word is one and the Son another, and the Word is not the Son, Baptism has no connection with the Word. How then are they able to hold that the Word is with the Father, when He is not with Him in the giving of Baptism? But perhaps they will say that in the Father's Name the Word is included? Wherefore then not the Spirit also? Or is the Spirit external to the Father? And the Man indeed (if the Word is not Son) is named after the Father, but the Spirit after the Man? And then the Monad, instead of dilating into a Triad, dilates according to them into a Tetrad, Father, Word, Son, and Holy Ghost. Being brought to shame on this ground, they have recourse to another, and say that not the Man by Himself whom the Lord bore, but both together, the Word and the Man, are the Son; for both joined together are named Son, as they say. Which then is cause of which? And which has made which a Son? Or, to speak more clearly, is the Word a Son because of the flesh? Or is the flesh called Son because of the Word? Or is neither the cause, but the concurrence of the two? If then the Word be a Son because of the flesh, of necessity the flesh is Son, and all those absurdities follow which have been already drawn from saying that the Man is Son. But if the flesh is called Son because of the Word, then even before the flesh the Word certainly, being such, was Son. For how could a being make other sons, not being himself a son, especially when there was a father? If then He makes sons for

Himself, then is He Himself Father; but if for the Father, then must He be Son, or rather that Son, by reason of Whom the rest are made sons.

If Christ and the Holy Spirit are but creatures made by God, then we are baptized in the name of God and two creatures and are not saved; we end up not only worshiping two creatures as divine but also become dependent on creatures rather than God for our salvation. "For the Arians do not baptize into Father and Son, but into Creator and creature, and into Maker and work." Again, liturgy, soteriology, and the doctrine of God come together into a synthesis so "that the right faith might follow upon learning, and together with faith might come the consecration of Baptism."

A similar point is made later by Basil of Caesarea (d. 379) in his *De Spiritu Sancto* (*On the Holy Spirit*),[71] where, against some semi-Arians who were asserting that baptism in the name of God alone was sufficient, he argues:

> 12.28. Let no one be misled by the fact of the apostle's frequently omitting the name of the Father and of the Holy Spirit when making mention of baptism, or on this account imagine that the invocation of the names is not observed. As many of you, he says, as were baptized into Christ have put on Christ; and again, As many of you as were baptized into Christ were baptized into his death. For the naming of Christ is the confession of the whole, showing forth as it does the God who gave, the Son who received, and the Spirit who is the unction. So we have learned from Peter, in the Acts, of Jesus of Nazareth whom God anointed with the Holy Ghost; Acts 10:38 and in Isaiah, The Spirit of the Lord is upon me, because the Lord has anointed me; Isaiah 60:1 and the Psalmist, Therefore God, even your God, has anointed you with the oil of gladness above your fellows. Scripture, however, in the case of baptism, sometimes plainly mentions the Spirit alone.
>
> For into one Spirit, it says, we were all baptized in one body. And in harmony with this are the passages: You shall be baptized with the Holy Ghost, Acts 1:5 and He shall baptize you with the Holy Ghost. Luke 3:16 But no one on this account would be justified in calling that baptism a perfect baptism wherein only the name of the Spirit was invoked. For the tradition that has been given us by the quickening

---

[71] NPNF, 4, 2nd series, pp. 3, 18, and 43.

grace must remain for ever inviolate. He who redeemed our life from destruction gave us power of renewal, whereof the cause is ineffable and hidden in mystery, but bringing great salvation to our souls, so that to add or to take away anything involves manifestly a falling away from the life everlasting. If then in baptism the separation of the Spirit from the Father and the Son is perilous to the baptizer, and of no advantage to the baptized, how can the rending asunder of the Spirit from Father and from Son be safe for us? Faith and baptism are two kindred and inseparable ways of salvation: faith is perfected through baptism, baptism is established through faith, and both are completed by the same names. For as we believe in the Father and the Son and the Holy Ghost, so are we also baptized in the name of the Father and of the Son and of the Holy Ghost; first comes the confession, introducing us to salvation, and baptism follows, setting the seal upon our assent.

Like Athanasius, Basil too appears to be referring to the trinitarian formula in baptism ("For as we believe in the Father and the Son and the Holy Ghost, so are we also baptized in the name of the Father and of the Son and of the Holy Ghost"). But much more is at stake in the relationship between baptism and the divinity of the Holy Spirit than the trinitarian baptismal formula and that "more" is precisely the profession of faith in Father, Son, and Holy Spirit. While the use of the trinitarian formula in baptism was certainly known by the early Syrian tradition, where it first appeared; by Athanasius in Egypt; by Basil and the other "Cappadocian Fathers," namely, Gregory of Nazianzus and Gregory of Nyssa; and clearly by the Antiochene theologians John Chrysostom and Theodore of Mopsuestia,[72] it was not regularly used in the West until the early Middle Ages. Indeed, what constituted the "formula" in the West, and for that matter earlier in Egypt as well, were three creedal questions and answers ("Do you believe in God, the Father . . . in Jesus Christ his Son our Lord . . . and in the Holy Spirit?") within the context of the conferral of baptism. In fact, it is these three baptismal interrogations that tended to develop in the West, at least, into what we eventually come to know as the Apostles' Creed, or the baptismal creed of the church at Rome, though

[72] See my *The Rites of Christian Initiation: Their Evolution and Interpretation*, 2nd rev. and exp. ed. (Collegeville, MN: Liturgical Press, Pueblo, 2007), 129–37.

used throughout the West (e.g., at Milan). In the East, similarly, what became eventually the Nicene-Constantinopolitan Creed itself was originally also a local baptismal creed of Syro-Palestinian origin (possibly Jerusalem or Antioch) with several anti-Arian clauses added.[73] For these Orthodox theologians, then, it is not simply the sacramental formulas used in baptism that function as a source for doctrine but the very trinitarian understanding of the tripartite profession of faith made in the context of baptism's conferral that becomes a doctrinal source. In other words, such liturgical language shapes even what will become the Orthodox creedal confession of faith. And, since the semi-Arians made essentially the same baptismal profession of faith in Father, Son, and Holy Spirit, and, at least in the East, used the same baptismal formula, the burden of proof was on them to demonstrate how their doctrinal positions could be defensible.

It is interesting to note here two other liturgical-sacramental aspects, however, that one might expect to have been significant but that do *not* appear to have played a role in this controversy. First, no one who emphasizes the Holy Spirit's divinity against the semi-Arian denial *ever* refers to a postbaptismal anointing or "Seal of the Holy Spirit" in doing so! Such absence, while admittedly an argument from silence, does suggest, nevertheless, additional evidence for those scholars who assert that, while a postbaptismal imposition with hands related to the gift of the Holy Spirit was known in the West from the time of Tertullian on, an explicit postbaptismal chrismation for the gift or Seal of the Spirit was a mid- to late fourth-century innovation in Eastern baptismal rites.[74] If this is correct, then it is the semi-Arian controversy itself that may have been the catalyst for this development. Hence, rather than the *lex orandi* shaping the *lex credendi*, to use the later terminology, it is the *lex credendi* that is shaping the *lex orandi*.

Second, there is similarly no evidence of anyone appealing to the various epicleses of the Holy Spirit in the prayers for the consecration

---

[73] See Berard Marthaler, *The Creed: The Apostolic Faith in Contemporary Theology* (Mystic, CT: Twenty-Third Publications, 1993), 90–93. On the development from interrogatory to declaratory creeds, see Liuwe H. Westra, *The Apostles' Creed: Origin, History, and Some Early Commentaries*, Instrumenta Patristica et Mediaevalia 43 (Turnhout: Brepols, 2002).

[74] Johnson, *The Rites of Christian Initiation*, 153ff.

of baptismal waters or within the eucharistic prayers in defense of the Spirit's divinity. In some of the Syrian texts quoted in the previous section, especially the Syrian *Acts of the Apostles* and the Anaphora of Addai and Mari, it is clear that there certainly were texts invoking the Holy Spirit in these liturgical rites. The Syrian *Didascalia Apostolorum* refers to the Eucharist being "accepted and sanctified by the Holy Spirit" and "sanctified by means of invocations."[75] To these examples may be added the epiclesis in the Egyptian (Sahidic Coptic) version of the Anaphora of St. Basil of Caesarea, called Egyptian Basil (or EgBAS), dated usually in the early fourth century and used still by the Coptic Orthodox Church:

> And we, sinners and unworthy and wretched, pray you, our God, in adoration that in the good pleasure of your goodness your Holy Spirit may descend upon us and upon these gifts that have been set before you, and may sanctify and make them holy of holies.[76]

The later version of this prayer, Byzantine Basil (or ByzBAS), most probably redacted by Basil of Caesarea himself and still used today in the Byzantine Rite, especially during Lent, expands upon the Spirit's role:

> And having set forth the likeness of the holy body and blood of your Christ, we pray and beseech you, O holy of holies, in the good pleasure of your bounty, that your [all-]Holy Spirit may come upon us and upon these gifts set forth, and bless them and sanctify and show (*he signs the holy gifts with the cross three times, saying:*) this bread the precious body of our Lord and God and Savior Jesus Christ. Amen. And this cup the precious blood of our Lord and God and Savior Jesus Christ, [Amen.] which is shed for the life of the world <and salvation> Amen <*thrice*>.[77]

While appeal could have been made to some of these earlier texts in defense of the Holy Spirit, Paul Bradshaw and I have suggested

---

[75] Sebastian Brock and Michael Vasey, *The Liturgical Portions of the* Didascalia, Grove Liturgical Study 29 (Cambridge, MA: Grove Books, 1982), 16, 32–33.
[76] PEER, 71.
[77] Ibid., 119–20.

elsewhere that anaphoral epicleses are moving from implicit to more explicit formulations in large part because of the specific development of an orthodox theology of the Holy Spirit.[78] That is, it is only natural that these fourth-century disputes over the relationship between the Holy Spirit to the Father and the Son would lead to an increased emphasis on a more explicit role of the Holy Spirit in liturgy. Here, then, like the postbaptismal chrismation as the "Seal of the Spirit," is another example of the inverse of the *lex orandi* principle. The development of trinitarian doctrine is further shaping the way in which the Holy Spirit is portrayed in the liturgy itself as the Spirit's "consecration" of the bread and cup moves from what Bradshaw and I refer to as an "Epiphany" focus—i.e., the Spirit is invoked to "show" or "reveal" Christ's Body and Blood—to an invocation related now to the Spirit invoked for explicitly "changing" or "making" the bread and wine into Christ's Body and Blood, as the following two examples from late fourth-century Jerusalem and Constantinople demonstrate. At Jerusalem, whatever the text of the eucharistic prayer known in the famous *Mystagogical Catecheses* of Bishop Cyril (or his successor John) may have been in the later fourth century, the theology of a Spirit epiclesis is even more explicit:

> Next, having sanctified ourselves with these spiritual hymns, we call on the merciful God to send the Holy Spirit on those things that are being presented, so that he may make the bread Christ's body and the wine Christ's blood; for clearly whatever the Holy Spirit touches is sanctified and transformed.[79]

And a similar development can be seen in the Anaphora of St. John Chrysostom (CHR), also like the role of Basil in the final version of ByzBAS, redacted by Chrysostom himself:

> We offer you also this reasonable and bloodless service, and we pray and beseech and entreat you, send down your Holy Spirit on us and on these gifts set forth; and make this bread the precious body of your Christ, [changing it by your Holy Spirit] Amen; and that which is in this cup the precious blood of your Christ, changing it by your

---

[78] Bradshaw and Johnson, *The Eucharistic Liturgies*, 121–23.
[79] PEER, 85–86.

Holy Spirit, Amen; so that they may become to those who partake
for vigilance of soul, for fellowship with the Holy Spirit, for the fullness of the kingdom (of heaven), for boldness toward you, not for
judgment or condemnation.[80]

Were such liturgical texts and their theological positions already widespread in the time period leading up to the Council of Constantinople,
it is hard to imagine that appeal would not have been made to them.
And, what is indeed fascinating in all this is that in his *De Spiritu Sancto*
27 Basil of Caesarea himself does refer to invocations (epicleses) over
the bread and cup in the Eucharist and the blessing of water and the
consecration of oil for chrismation in baptism.[81] But he does this simply
to refer to unwritten liturgical traditions versus written texts and in
no way to defend the role or divinity of the Holy Spirit.

What does become a liturgical issue, however, is the use of the trinitarian doxology in liturgical prayer, often at the conclusion of prayers
or attached to the end of psalms or hymns, either "Glory be to the
Father, *through* the Son, *in* the Holy Spirit," or "Glory be *to* the Father,
with the Son, together *with* the Holy Spirit," and/or "Glory be *to* the
Father, and *to* the Son, and *to* the Holy Spirit." The uncoordinated
form of the doxology (to, through, in), as noted at the beginning of
this chapter, was favored by Jungmann as a sign of antiquity consistent with Origen's description of Christian prayer as always *to* the
Father, *through* the Son, and *in* the Holy Spirit, although, as we have
also seen, Origen himself was anything but consistent in this position.

There is no question but that this uncoordinated form of the doxology and conclusion to prayer in general was widely known in early
Christian liturgical texts and that many, including the Arians and
semi-Arians, claimed this as authoritative and normative for praying. Indeed, one might say that it was the Arians or semi-Arians
who, a century before Prosper of Aquitaine, were already using the
lex orandi, lex credendi argument in defense of their doctrinal position
that the Son and the Holy Spirit were subordinate creatures made
by the one God, *through* whom and *in* whom prayer was offered. In

[80] Ibid., 133.
[81] If Basil knew a chrismation in baptism it was most likely, as in Chrysostom,
prebaptismal and not postbaptismal. See Johnson, *The Rites of Christian Initiation*, 134–37.

this sense, notes Catherine Mowry LaCugna, in clear dependence on Jungmann's approach, the Arians and Arian sympathizers "looked like the 'faithful conservatives.'"[82]

For Jungmann,[83] the coordinated form of the doxology originated at Antioch after 340, hence, after Nicea, because Bishop Leontius (344–358), an Arian sympathizer, was said to have muffled the doxology at the end of prayers in order to hide from the gathered assembly which form he was actually using. This conclusion regarding its origins, however, can no longer be held. Already in the Prayer of Polycarp noted above, whether second or third century in date, the coordinated form already appears:

> For this and for everything I praise thee, I bless thee, I glorify thee, through the eternal and heavenly High Priest, Jesus Christ, thy beloved Servant, through whom be glory *to thee with* (συν or *syn*) him *and the Holy Spirit* both now and unto the ages to come. Amen. [Emphasis added]

Similarly, Dionysius of Alexandria in the mid-third century writes the following in a letter to Dionysius of Rome:

> Having received from the presbyters who went before us a form and rule, we conclude our present letter to you with those words by which we, like them, make our (Eucharistic) thanksgiving: To God the Father and the Son our Lord Jesus Christ with (*syn*) the Holy Spirit be glory and might for ever and ever. Amen.[84]

And, for that matter, the beginning of the Anaphora of Addai and Mari, at least in its final form, has the following trinitarian reference in a coordinated form:

> Worthy of glory from every mouth and thanksgiving from every tongue is the adorable and glorious name of the Father and of the Son and of the Holy Spirit.

[82] Catherine Mowry LaCugna, *God for Us: The Trinity and Christian Life* (San Francisco: HarperCollins, 1991), 122.

[83] Jungmann, *The Place of Christ*, 195–200.

[84] Translation as cited by Geoffrey Wainwright, *Doxology: The Praise of God in Worship, Doctrine and Life* (New York: Oxford University Press, 1980), 96.

Of this, Bryan Spinks notes, "unless one is to maintain that any reference to Father, Son, and Spirit outside a baptismal context is 'late,' there is no reason why the Matthean triune names should not be regarded as original to this anaphora, which is almost certainly one of our earliest eucharistic prayers."[85]

Together with the assumption that the coordinated form of the doxology only came into existence at Antioch after 340, traditional scholarship also claimed that it was Basil of Caesarea who was responsible for the introduction of its use in late fourth-century Cappadocia. But Basil himself in his *De Spiritu Sancto* flatly denies this and, in fact, notes that both forms of the doxology are used regularly in his liturgies.

> 1.3. Lately when praying with the people, and using the full doxology to God the Father in both forms, at one time *with* the Son *together with* the Holy Ghost, and at another *through* the Son *in* the Holy Ghost, I was attacked by some of those present on the ground that I was introducing novel and at the same time mutually contradictory terms. You, however, chiefly with the view of benefiting them, or, if they are wholly incurable, for the security of such as may fall in with them, have expressed the opinion that some clear instruction ought to be published concerning the force underlying the syllables employed. I will therefore write as concisely as possible, in the endeavor to lay down some admitted principle for the discussion.

And, in response to those who wanted *written* evidence for the coordinated form he directs attention once again to the confession of trinitarian faith in baptism:

> 27.67. Time will fail me if I attempt to recount the unwritten mysteries of the Church. Of the rest I say nothing; but of the very confession of our faith in Father, Son, and Holy Ghost, what is the written source? If it be granted that, as we are baptized, so also under the obligation to believe, we make our confession in like terms as our baptism, in accordance with the tradition of our baptism and in conformity with the principles of true religion, let our opponents grant us too the right to be as consistent in our ascription of glory as in our confession of faith. If they deprecate our doxology on the ground that it lacks written

---

[85] Spinks, "The Place of Christ," 10–11.

authority, let them give us the written evidence for the confession of our faith and the other matters which we have enumerated. While the unwritten traditions are so many, and their bearing on the mystery of godliness (1 Timothy 3:16) is so important, can they refuse to allow us a single word which has come down to us from the Fathers;—which we found, derived from untutored custom, abiding in unperverted churches;—a word for which the arguments are strong, and which contributes in no small degree to the completeness of the force of the mystery?[86]

Somewhat later in history, Ambrose in *De Sacramentis* 2.20 takes a similar position against the Arians in his address to the neophytes in Milan:

Do not be surprised that we are baptized in one name: in the name, that is, of the Father and of the Son and of the Holy Spirit; because Christ spoke of only one name where there is one substance, one divinity, one majesty. This is the name of which it is written: "In this must all find salvation." It is in this name that you have all been saved, that you have been restored to the grace of life.[87]

It is Basil, however, who offers the most spirited defense of the coordinated form of the doxology. In so doing he provides evidence of its traditional usage by pointing to the mid-third-century letter of Dionysius of Alexandria we saw above (*De Spiritu Sancto* 29.72), to the inability of the Syriac-speaking churches in "Mesopotamia" to use anything other than the coordinated form of the doxology on linguistic grounds (*De Spiritu Sancto* 29.74), and to the doxology of the Vespers lamp-lighting hymn, *Phôs Hilaron* ("O Joyous Light"), a hymn that Basil considers already to be ancient and of unknown authorship (*De Spiritu Sancto* 29.73). The final form of this hymn, still used daily in Byzantine Vespers and adopted by many diverse liturgical traditions in our own day, reads:

[86] NPNF, 4, 2nd series, 43.

[87] Translation from Edward Yarnold, *The Awe-Inspiring Rites of Initiation*, 2nd ed. (Collegeville, MN: Liturgical Press, 2001), 118. See also Ambrose, *De mysteriis* 5.28. Theodore of Mopsuestia in northern Syria makes a similar statement in his own baptismal catecheses. See his *Baptismal Homilies* 3.16.

> O joyous light, of the holy glory of the immortal Father,
>   Heavenly, holy, blessed Jesus Christ!
> Having come to the setting of the sun, and beholding the
>   Evening light,
> We praise God Father, Son and Holy Spirit!
> It is fitting at all times that you be praised with auspicious voices,
>   O Son of God, giver of life;
> Wherefore the whole world glorifies you![88]

Further, with regard to both forms of the doxology themselves, Basil demonstrates how each of them is to be regarded as an orthodox expression of trinitarian faith:

> 27.68. I will proceed to state once more wherein they [both forms of the doxology] agree and wherein they differ from one another;—not that they are opposed in mutual antagonism, but that each contributes its own meaning to true religion. The preposition "in" states the truth rather relatively to ourselves; while "with" proclaims the fellowship of the Spirit with God. Wherefore we use both words, by the one expressing the dignity of the Spirit; by the other announcing the grace that is with us. Thus we ascribe glory to God both in the Spirit, and with the Spirit; and herein it is not our word that we use, but we follow the teaching of the Lord as we might a fixed rule, and transfer His word to things connected and closely related, and of which the conjunction in the mysteries is necessary. We have deemed ourselves under a necessary obligation to combine in our confession of the faith Him who is numbered with Them at Baptism, and we have treated the confession of the faith as the origin and parent of the doxology. What, then, is to be done? They must now instruct us either not to baptize as we have received, or not to believe as we were baptized, or not to ascribe glory as we have believed. Let any man prove if he can that the relation of sequence in these acts is not necessary and unbroken; or let any man deny if he can that innovation here must mean ruin everywhere. Yet they never stop dinning in our ears that the ascription of glory with the Holy Spirit is unauthorized and unscriptural and the like. We have stated that so far as the sense goes it is the same

---

[88] Translation from Antonia Tripolitis, "PHOS HILARON: Ancient Hymn and Modern Enigma," *Vigiliae christianae* 24 (1970): 189, as adapted and cited by Robert Taft, "Christ in the Byzantine Divine Office," in Spinks, *The Place of Christ in Liturgical Prayer*, 74.

to say glory be to the Father and to the Son and to the Holy Ghost, and glory be to the Father and to the Son with the Holy Ghost. It is impossible for any one to reject or cancel the syllable "and," which is derived from the very words of our Lord, and there is nothing to hinder the acceptance of its equivalent. What amount of difference and similarity there is between the two we have already shown. And our argument is confirmed by the fact that the Apostle uses either word indifferently,—saying at one time in the name of the Lord Jesus and by the Spirit of our God; [1 Cor 6:11] at another when you are gathered together, and my Spirit, with the power of our Lord Jesus, [1 Cor 5:4] with no idea that it makes any difference to the connection of the names whether he use the conjunction or the preposition.[89]

In this brilliant defense of the orthodoxy of both forms Basil is responsible for a distinction that will become classic in trinitarian theology, the inseparable relationship between what LaCugna refers to as *theologia* and *oikonomia*, between the "economic" and the "immanent" Trinity, or between God's Being and God's Act. That is, if the uncoordinated form of the doxology is used, we are referring to how God acts in the *oikonomia* for human salvation since all divine acting begins with the Father, is expressed in the Son, and comes to fruition among us in the Spirit. And if this triune way is the way of all divine acting, then this must be how God is *in se*, in God's very being. God is what God does. Hence, the coordinate form of the doxology expresses this true *theologia*, the ontology of God, God's very being, and glory is thus given equally to Father, Son, and Holy Spirit. Both are orthodox since both express the same reality from two different perspectives. LaCugna writes that for Basil and for orthodox trinitarian theology in general:

> In the liturgical context, a right understanding of the distinction between the order of salvation (*oikonomia*) and the order of God's eternal being (*theologia*) is crucial. The apparent subordinationism of some doxologies reflects the order of salvation history; no inequality is implied at the level of the being of Father, Son, and Spirit. . . . Basil's opponents drew the wrong conclusion, namely, that if Christ is our way back to God, Christ is inferior to God; or if the Spirit is our way to Christ, the Spirit is less than Christ and also less than the Father. For Basil, as for all orthodox theologians to follow, it was of utmost

[89] NPNF, 8, 2nd series, 43.

importance to show that to worship the God of Jesus Christ in the [uncoordinated] doxology was the same as to worship *God as such,* in whom there is neither subordination nor inequality of persons.[90]

Basil of Caesarea himself did not live to see the fruits of his work on the divinity of the Holy Spirit, a claim he could not make explicit due to political circumstances at the time. Nevertheless, it is his own baptismal and doxological defense of the Holy Spirit, together with the more philosophical approaches of Gregory of Nyssa and Gregory of Nazianzus on the procession of the Holy Spirit from the Father, that will come to be enshrined in the language about the Holy Spirit at the Council of Constantinople (381 CE, two years after Basil's death) and, hence, in the final version of the Nicene-Constantinopolitan Creed. To profess in the creed that it is the Holy Spirit "Who is worshiped [*proskynoumenon*] and glorified [*syndoxazomenon*] together with the Father and the Son" is due to the liturgical arguments advanced by both Athanasius of Alexandria and Basil of Caesarea.

Another liturgical element that certainly needs to be considered in this context as well is the relationship between the classic January 6 feast of the Epiphany, at least in the East, and the newly emerging feast of the December 25 Christmas.[91] Traditional scholarship, represented especially by Anton Baumstark and Bernard Botte, claimed that the adoption of the December 25 feast, known in Rome by 335, was a deliberate anti-Arian move focusing on defending the preexistence and incarnation of the *Logos.* And there can be no question that in places like Cappadocia Nicene and Constantinopolitan orthodox trinitarian and christological concerns played a strong role in the celebration of both December 25 and January 6.[92] While this does not mean necessarily that the adoption of Christmas and Epiphany came about for doctrinal reasons in the East, it does underscore the use of the content of these feasts for promoting and defending Orthodox dogma.

[90] LaCugna, *God for Us,* 120–21. See also Wainwright, *Doxology,* 100ff.

[91] On all of this, see Paul F. Bradshaw and Maxwell E. Johnson, *The Origins of Feasts, Fasts, and Seasons in Early Christianity,* Alcuin Club Collections 86 (London: SPCK; Collegeville, MN: Liturgical Press, Pueblo, 2011), 123–57.

[92] See Jill Burnett Comings, *Aspects of the Liturgical Year in Cappadocia (325–430),* Patristic Studies 7 (New York: Lang, 2005), 87–90.

The real dogmatic concerns with Epiphany and Christmas, however, have to do with what appears to be the separation of Jesus' birth from his baptism on January 6 in the East. That is, contemporary scholarship on Epiphany in the East, viewing January 6, like December 25 in the West, as a feast of Jesus' "beginnings" at the head of the year, has enabled us to see that christological issues are part of the mix with Epiphany or Theophany from the start. That is, our earliest witnesses to Epiphany, Clement of Alexandria in Egypt as well as the Syrian sources studied by Gabriele Winkler,[93] demonstrate that Jesus' birth and baptism were celebrated together originally with his baptism functioning as his "spiritual birth" in the Jordan, underscored by the citation of Psalm 2:7, "You are my son; today I have begotten you," as the words of the divine voice to Jesus at that event, rather than "You are my Son, the Beloved; with you I am well pleased" (see Luke 3:22). At the same time that the separation of Jesus' birth and baptism into the distinct feasts of Christmas and Epiphany is taking place, both now concerned with the *revelation* of his divine identity either at Bethlehem or at the Jordan, we are right in the midst of the great trinitarian and christological debates summarized above and we are precisely in that moment of history when, shortly after the Council of Nicea, baptism at Easter is becoming the theoretical, but certainly not the practical, norm in both East and West and, hence, replacing what had been a practice of baptism at Epiphany in Egypt, Jerusalem, Cappadocia, and probably Syria. Therefore, as a result of later christological development in the church, together with the eventual acceptance of the December 25 Christmas in the East, the apparent Adoptionist overtones of the earlier theology of Jesus' pneumatic "birth" in the Jordan were suppressed (i.e., Jesus "becomes" or is "adopted" by God at his baptism), overtones that would have appealed greatly to the Arian theological position, and a reinterpretation of Epiphany not as the "birth" of Christ in the Jordan but as a commemoration of his baptism alone resulted.

---

[93] Gabriele Winkler, "The Appearance of the Light at the Baptism of Jesus and the Origins of the Feast of Epiphany," in *Between Memory and Hope: Readings on the Liturgical Year*, ed. Maxwell E. Johnson (Collegeville, MN: Liturgical Press, 2000), 291–348.

3. Conclusion

One of the principles for liturgical-historical study developed by Paul Bradshaw in his work on early Christian liturgy is that "the so-called Constantinian revolution served as much to intensify existing trends as it did to initiate new ones,"[94] that is, the liturgical changes in the mid- to late fourth century are as much about "evolution" as they are about radical changes. As we have seen in this chapter, "evolution" is clearly the case with regard to the liturgical underpinning of what becomes orthodox Christology and trinitarian theology. What distinguished Christianity from the beginning is its inclusion of Christ in the worship of God and, indeed, the worship of Christ himself, a worship that is expressed in numerous prayers—liturgical and otherwise—throughout the first three centuries of the church's existence. Similarly, if in the earliest period the distinction between Christ (or the Logos) and the Holy Spirit was not all that clear within what might be called a "Binitarian" theological approach, the presence of the Holy Spirit in baptism—whether by means of a trinitarian formula or a threefold interrogation about belief in Father, Son, and Holy Spirit—and the known existence of doxologies giving equal glory to all three Persons, will certainly contribute to the trinitarian doctrine of God as that comes to be expressed in the Nicene-Constantinopolitan Creed. And, thanks to Athanasius and Basil, it is the baptismal liturgy and the liturgical doxologies that come to the fore in this development, underscoring again the importance of liturgical prayer and liturgy in general for the shaping of doctrine. This focus on evolution and continuity rather than revolution or discontinuity as it applies to the liturgical influence on the development of doctrine is well expressed by Wainwright when he asks, especially in relation to liturgical (baptismal) and other texts, "does not all this in the long run *imply* the position which Athanasius and Basil will make explicit?" And, further:

> As in christology, so in pneumatology, it was human salvation that is at stake. . . . To the extent that God engages *himself* with the world,

---

[94] Paul F. Bradshaw, *The Search for the Origins of Christian Worship*, 1st ed. (New York: Oxford, 1992), 65. The quote does not appear in the second, revised edition (London: SPCK, 2002), but the same idea is expressed on 211–12.

it is legitimate to read back from his presence and action into his very being. If he appears to engage himself with the world *in different ways*, it will to that extent be legitimate to trace a certain plurality into God himself.[95]

Finally, this chapter has provided an occasional critique of traditional scholarship, especially as represented by the classic studies of Joseph Jungmann on this topic. But it is important to note that even if Jungmann ruled out of consideration early liturgical evidence that needs to be included, he still has an important point to make. That is, if the coordinated form of the doxology is ancient and if the uncoordinated form can be considered orthodox by Basil, it is true, nevertheless, that following the Council of Constantinople, especially within the further development of Christology, the uncoordinated form of the doxology will either become omitted or be brought into harmony with the coordinated form (e.g., "*through* Christ, *with* whom and *with* the Holy Spirit be glory). While such phrasing is perfectly orthodox, it is true that there is a loss of the theology of Christ the High Priest and Mediator precisely in his humanity in both East and West. This will be explored more fully in the final chapter of this study.

---

[95] Wainwright, *Doxology*, 100 (emphasis is original).

Chapter 3

Christ and Mary

The church's liturgical and other prayer, as we saw in the previous chapter, played a significant role in the development of the doctrine of the Trinity at the councils of Nicea and Constantinople. The question this chapter addresses is whether and to what extent the same claim might be made for the next two ecumenical councils of Ephesus (431 CE) and Chalcedon (451 CE), which dealt with further christological issues in coming to formulations about the relationship of Christ's human and divine natures. On the one hand, the question is rather moot since these councils obviously are not concerned with the question of worshiping Christ or glorifying the Holy Spirit equally with the Father and, in fact, the Nicene-Constantinopolitan Creed had made that liturgical practice part of Orthodox doctrine already. Hence, the issues here might be said to be more doctrinal and philosophical than liturgical.

On the other hand, the liturgical and devotional question does come to the fore with the christological title officially given to the Virgin Mary at Ephesus, *Theotokos* (God-Bearer), and, together with the christological formula of "one Person, two natures" adopted at Chalcedon, there are certainly liturgical implications. Thus, the term *Theotokos* as a product of the church's worship and precisely those liturgical implications of these christological decisions are the emphases that will shape the focus of this chapter.

1. Mary as *Theotokos* (God-Bearer)

The fathers gathered at the Church of St. Mary in Ephesus accepted as doctrinally Orthodox the following letter of Cyril of Alexandria to and against Nestorius of Constantinople, whose controversial theological position against calling Mary the *Theotokos* was the catalyst for the council itself:

We must not, therefore, divide the one Lord Jesus Christ into two Sons. Neither will it at all avail to a sound faith to hold, as some do, a union of persons; for the Scripture has not said that the Word united to himself the person of man, but that he was made flesh. This expression, however, "the Word was made flesh," can mean nothing else but that he partook of flesh and blood like to us; he made our body his own, and came forth man from a woman, not casting off his existence as God, or his generation of God the Father, but even in taking to himself flesh remaining what he was. This the declaration of the correct faith proclaims everywhere. This was the sentiment of the holy Fathers; therefore they ventured to call the holy Virgin, the Mother of God, not as if the nature of the Word or his divinity had its beginning from the holy Virgin, but because of her was born that holy body with a rational soul, to which the Word being personally united is said to be born according to the flesh. These things, therefore, I now write unto you for the love of Christ, beseeching you as a brother, and testifying to you before Christ and the elect angels, that you would both think and teach these things with us, that the peace of the Churches may be preserved and the bond of concord and love continue unbroken amongst the Priests of God.[1]

And the first of the twelve anathemas adopted by the council, and suggested by Cyril himself, states, "if anyone does not confess that Emmanuel is God in truth, and therefore that the holy virgin is the mother of God (for she bore in a fleshly way the Word of God become flesh), let him be anathema."[2]

Because the term has become so bound up with the christological concerns of Ephesus, it has become common to treat the question of the *Theotokos* and devotion to the *Theotokos* as a fifth-century doctrinal issue that gives rise to increased devotion with little or no attention to its wider context or possible prehistory. A summary statement by Elizabeth Johnson in her recent study, *Truly Our Sister: A Theology of Mary in the Communion of Saints*, well illustrates this point:

---

[1] Cyril., *Opera*, Tom. X.; *Epist*. iv., col. 43. Translation from NPNF, 14, series 2.

[2] Text cited in Philip Jenkins, *The Jesus Wars: How Four Patriarchs, Three Queens, and Two Emperors Decided What Christians Would Believe for the Next 1,500 Years* (New York: HarperOne, 2010), 165.

[T]he school of Alexandria argued for a stronger, ontological form of union in which the divine Son of God personally united himself to human nature. While safeguarding the unity of natures in the person of Christ, this notion tended to dilute his humanity, seeing it as somehow mixed with or swallowed up by transcendent divinity. In this school, the passionately preferred title for Mary was *Theotokos*, or God-bearer, meaning that she was the mother of the one who is personally the Word of God. Although the essence of the controversy was christological, the marian title itself bore the brunt of the dispute. When the Council of Ephesus in 431 opted for the title *Theotokos*, it spread like wildfire, keeping its original form in the East and being transmuted into the more colloquial "Mother of God" in the West. According to most scholars, the impetus from this council allowed the development of the marian cult to go public in the church. Although discourse about Mary had been in play to express christological truths, it opened up the later trajectory where attention was focused on Mary herself.[3]

Given this claim, it would seem that the very question of the origins of the title itself would seem to be of great importance for historical and liturgical-theological scholarship. Is the title of *Theotokos* devotional and/or liturgical in emphasis before it even emerges as a particular dogmatic term, a development perhaps out of the church's *lex orandi* broadly understood? Indeed, are we dealing here with a development that constitutes a "revolution" in doctrine, piety, and devotion or one that, again as in the previous chapter, is merely reflecting an evolution consistent with what went before?

In his 1996 study, *Mary through the Centuries: Her Place in the History of Culture*, Jaroslav Pelikan notes not only that the origins of the term *Theotokos* are obscure, though "an original Christian creation," but also that "the first completely authenticated instances of the use of this title came from the city of Athanasius, Alexandria. Alexander, [Athanasius'] patron, referred to Mary as Theotokos in his encyclical of circa 319 about the heresy of Arius."[4] That it is also a common enough term

---

[3] Elizabeth Johnson, *Truly Our Sister: A Theology of Mary in the Communion of Saints* (New York/London: Continuum, 2003), 117–18.

[4] Jaroslav Pelikan, *Mary through the Centuries: Her Place in the History of Culture* (New Haven and London: Yale University Press, 1996), 57. While Pelikan is surely correct in noting that the title *Theotokos* was "a term of Christian coinage" and

in the writings and theology of Athanasius himself is confirmed by a word search in the *Thesaurus Linguae Graecae* (hereafter, TLG), which reveals that, together with numerous spurious attributions, *Theotokos* appears four times in his *Orationes tres contra Arianos*, once in his *Vita Antonii*, three times in *Expositiones in Psalmos*, and at least once in *De Incarnatione Verbi Dei*.

If both Alexander and Athanasius use the term in an overall anti-Arian context, however, the term itself is not used in its later sense to defend a particular christological assertion about the unity of natures or personhood in Christ, which is certainly the meaning of the term at Ephesus. In his encyclical letter to Alexander of Constantinople, Alexander writes only that Christ "bore a body not in appearance but in truth, derived from Mary the Mother of God [ἐκ τῆς θεοτόκου Μαρίας]."[5] And in *De Incarnatione Verbi Dei* Athansius writes, "The Word begotten of the Father from on high, inexpressibly, inexplicably, incomprehensibly and eternally, is He that is born in time here below of the Virgin Mary, the Mother of God [ἐκ παρθένου θεοτόκου Μαρίας]."[6] In both cases it would seem that the term is used as little more than an honorific title for Mary. That is, the apparent anti-Docetic defense of Christ's humanity, "not in appearance but in truth," or the temporal birth of the *Word* does not need the term *Theotokos* to demonstrate or defend this assertion since a simple reference to the Virgin Mary without an additional title would have been sufficient.

That in the time period of the mid- to late fourth century the term *Theotokos* was generally used in this sense of a widespread title without

---

not borrowed from pagan use, it remains true as well that in the world of early Christianity devotion to mother goddesses like Isis, whose cult is first testified to also in Alexandria (see Theodor Klauser, "Rom und der Kult der Gottesmutter Maria," *Jahrbuch für Antike und Christentum* 15 [1972]: 120), or to "mothers of the gods," such as the shrine to the Μήτηρ θεῶν in pre-Christian Constantinople (see Nicholas Constas, "Weaving the Body of God: Proclus of Constantinople, the Theotokos, and the Loom of the Flesh," *Journal of Early Christian Studies* 3, no. 2 [1995]: 174n21), was part of the overall cultural landscape. That such a cultural context would be influential in shaping popular marian piety seems rather obvious.

[5] PG 18:568. Translation from Pelikan, *Mary through the Centuries*, 237.

[6] *De Incarnatione* 8, PG 26. Translation from William A. Jurgens, *The Faith of the Early Fathers*, vol. 1 (Collegeville, MN: Liturgical Press, 1970), 340.

necessarily implying a *particular* christological or doctrinal position is the conclusion of Marek Starowieyski in his compelling 1989 essay, "Le titre Θεοτόκος avant le concile d'Ephèse."[7] Herein Starowieyski provides an impressive list of fourth-century and early (pre-Ephesian) fifth-century authors where the title appears. In addition to Alexander and Athanasius, of course, this list includes the Synod of Antioch; Arius of Alexandria; Eustathius of Antioch; Eusebius of Caesarea; Asterius Sophistes; Hegemonius; Julian the Apostate; Titus of Bostra; Basil the Great; Cyril of Jerusalem; Apollinaris of Laodicea; Gregory Nazianzen; Gregory of Nyssa; Eunomius; Diodore of Tarsus; Didymus the Blind; Epiphanius; Antiochus of Ptolemais; Severian of Gabala; Theophilus of Alexandria; Theodore of Mopsuestia; Nilus of Ancyra; various pseudonymous treatises attributed to Athanasius, Chrysostom, and Ephrem the Syrian; and Ambrose of Milan, cited as the first to use the term *"Mater Dei"* in the Latin church.[8] Since this list includes Orthodox, Arian, Arianizing, Apollinarist, and anti-Apollinarist authors, Starowieyski rightly concludes that:

> The term is employed, it seems, with no accord to their respective christologies. This title has no repercussions on their theology, nor their theologies on the title. The texts come from Egypt (certainly the greater number), from Palestine, Syria, Mesopotamia, Arabia, and Asia Minor. Its use is thus general in the Mediterranean region. In taking the context into consideration, it is certain that the title is only employed as a simple appellation, with the exception of texts from the end of the fourth century.[9]

In the first quarter of the fourth century, therefore, i.e., about one hundred years *before* the Council of Ephesus itself, the term *Theotokos* had become—or was becoming—a common title for the Virgin Mary. But how far back does its use go before this?

---

[7] Marek Starowieyski, "Le titre Θεοτόκος avant le concile d'Ephèse," *Studia Patristica* 19 (1989): 236–42. Two other now standard reference works on early Mariology should be consulted: *Mary: The Complete Resource*, ed. Sarah Jane Boss (New York: Oxford University Press, 2007), 11–148; and *The Origins of the Cult of the Virgin Mary*, ed. Chris Maunder (New York: Burns & Oates, 2008).

[8] For the full list and texts see Starowieyski, "Le titre Θεοτόκος," 237–38.

[9] Ibid., 238.

Some contemporary biblical scholars would push the evidence for the idea, if not the title itself, back into the New Testament infancy narratives, where, at least, Elizabeth's designation of Mary as "Mother of my Lord" (Luke 1:43) may well mean "Mother of Yahweh!"[10] Similarly, Ignatius of Antioch, in his letter to the Ephesians says that "our *God*, Jesus the Christ, was conceived by Mary by the dispensation of God."[11] And by the beginning of the third century the word Μήτηρ in reference to Mary was starting to appear in an abbreviated form (MR) as a *nomen sacrum* in New Testament papyri.[12] At the end of the third and beginning of the fourth century the word may have appeared in a lost treatise of Pierius (d. 309) called περί τῆς θεοτόκου,[13] and in a fragment attributed to Peter of Alexandria.[14]

2. The *Theotokos* in Early Christian Liturgy and Devotion

Starowieyski also includes in his list of references the anaphora called Egyptian or Alexandrian Basil (hereafter EgBAS), one of our earliest surviving eucharistic prayers often dated in the first part of the fourth century. Significantly, while much of the extant text is available only in the later Bohairic Coptic dialect, the Sahidic version edited by J. Doresse and E. Lanne also contains this important text from the intercessions:

> Since, Master, it is a command of your only-begotten Son that we should share in the commemoration of your saints, vouchsafe to remember, Lord, those of our fathers who have been pleasing to you from eternity: patriarchs, prophets, apostles, martyrs, confessors, preachers, evangelists, and all the righteous perfected in faith; especially at all times the holy and glorious Mary, Mother of God; and by her prayers have mercy on us all, and save us through your holy name which has been invoked upon us.[15]

[10] See C. Kavin Rowe, "Luke and the Trinity: An Essay in Ecclesial Biblical Theology," *Scottish Journal of Theology* 56 (2003): 1–26.

[11] Ignatius, *Eph.* 18 (emphasis added). See also, *Eph.* 7 and 19.

[12] A. H. R. E. Paap, *Nomina Sacra in the Greek Papyri of the First Five Centuries* (Leiden: E. J. Brill, 1959), 15.

[13] See J. Quasten, *Patrology*, vol. 2 (Westminster: Newman Press, 1953), 112.

[14] Fragment 7, PG 18:517B.

[15] Text in J. Doresse and E. Lanne, *Un témoin archaïque de la liturgie copte de saint Basile* (Louvain: Publications Universitaires, 1960); and J. R. K. Fenwick, *The*

In the Armenian version of Basil (hereafter ArmBAS), apart from the inclusion of the names of John the Baptist and Saint Stephen the Protomartyr,[16] after "the Mother of God, the holy Virgin Mary," the text does not ask for mercy by her prayers—or by anyone else's—but refers simply to all the saints who are remembered or commemorated in the Eucharist.[17]

It is necessary to proceed here with the utmost caution. In her study of the intercessions in the Anaphora of John Chrysostom (hereafter CHR), Gabriele Winkler has argued, based on early anaphoral sources (i.e., Strasbourg papyrus, *Apostolic Constitutions* 8, and Cyril (John) of Jerusalem's *Mystagogical Catechesis* 5) that the evolution of the anaphoral commemoration of the saints evolved from listing only categories of saints (patriarchs, prophets, apostles, and martyrs) to naming specific saints, with Mary herself added only later as a result

---

Anaphoras of St. Basil and St. James: An Investigation into Their Common Origin, Orientalia Christiana Analecta 240 (Rome: Pontificium Istituto Orientale, 1992), 26. Translation from PEER, 72.

[16] H. Engberding noted that the inclusion of St. Stephen was due to the influence of the Anaphora of James. See H. Engberding, "Das anaphorische Fürbittgebet der syrischen Basiliusliturgie," *Oriens Christianus* 45 (1966): 16. In addition to this essay, on the intercessions in the Basilian anaphoras in general, see idem, "Das anaphorische Fürbittgebet der Basiliusliturgie," *Oriens Christianus* 47 (1963): 16–52; "Das anaphorische Fürbittgebet der Basiliusliturgie," *Oriens Christianus* 49 (1965): 18–37, esp. 26–27; and "Das anaphorische Fürbittgebet der armenischen Basiliusliturgie," *Oriens Christianus* 51 (1967): 29–50.

[17] For the text in Armenian with German translation, see E. Renhart, "Die älteste armenische Anaphora," in *Armenische Liturgien: Ein Blick auf eine ferne christliche Kultur*, ed. E. Renhart and J. Dum-Tragut (Graz-Salzburg: Schnider Verlag, 2001), 172–73. Although since H. Engberding's magisterial study, *Das eucharistische Hochgebet der Basileiosliturgie* (Münster: Aschendorff, 1931), most contemporary liturgical scholarship has viewed EgBAS as the earliest extant version of the Basilian anaphoral tradition, Gabriele Winkler has drawn recent attention to the importance of ArmBAS and has suggested a Syrian rather than Cappadocian origin for this widespread and influential eucharistic prayer. See her *Die Basilius-Anaphora: Edition der beiden armenischen Redaktionen und der relevanten Fragmente, Übersetzung und Zusammenschau aller Versionen im Licht der orientalischen Überlieferungen*, Anaphorae Orientales 2 (Rome: Pontificio Istituto Orientale, 2005). It may certainly be the case, then, that this particular commemoration of the *Theotokos* is yet another example of the antiquity of ArmBAS.

of the christological controversies.[18] In CHR the "commemoration" is part of the anamnesis/offering, not the intercessions, and reads, "We offer you this reasonable service also for (ὑπὲρ) those who rest in faith, . . . especially our all-holy, immaculate, highly glorious, Blessed Lady, Mother of God and ever-Virgin Mary."[19] And of this "Theotokos ekphonesis" Robert Taft has written that it is "but the incipit of the now defunct diptychs of the dead. Its interpolation into both the [Byz] Basil and Chrysostom Anaphoras occurred under Patriarch Gennadius I (458–471), at the command of Emperor Leo I (457–474), an innovation provoked by Patriarch Martyrius (459–470) of Antioch's refusal to grant Mary the Theotokos title."[20]

It should also be noted that the reference to the *Theotokos* both in ByzBAS and CHR with the addition of several honorific adjectives (i.e., "*all*-holy, immaculate, highly blessed (glorious), Blessed Lady") is expanded in relation to EgBAS; ArmBAS, as well as Syrian Basil;[21] and the Antiochene Syriac anaphora called the Twelve Apostles (hereafter APsyr), which has a close familial relationship to CHR. The pertinent text from APsyr reads, "Especially therefore let us make the memorial of the holy Mother of God and ever-Virgin Mary," and, after listing apostles, prophets, and saints, continues in a manner akin to EgBAS, "by whose prayers and supplications may we be preserved from evil, and may mercy be upon us in either world."[22] Interestingly enough, though without reference to the *Theotokos*, the author of *Mystagogical Catechesis* 5.9, in describing the commemoration of patriarchs, prophets, apostles, and martyrs in the fourth-century Jerusalem anaphora, includes the phrase "that

[18] G. Winkler, "Die Interzession der Chrysostomusanaphora in ihrer geschichtliche Entwicklung," *Orientalia Christiana Periodica* 36 (1970): 309ff.

[19] PEER, 133.

[20] R. Taft, "Prayer to or for the Saints? A Note on the Sanctoral Intercessions/ Commemorations in the Anaphora," in *Ab Oriente et Occidente (Mt 8, 11): Kirche aus Ost und West: Gendenkschrift für Wilhelm Nyssen* (Erzabtei St. Ottilien: Eos Verlag, 1996), 440. See also idem, *A History of the Liturgy of St. John Chrysostom*, vol. 4: *The Diptychs*, Orientalia Christiana Analecta 238 (Rome: Pontificio Istituto Orientale, 1991), 100–102.

[21] H. Engberding, "Das anaphorische Fürbittgebet der syrischen Basiliusliturgie," *Oriens Christianus* 50 (1966): 16.

[22] PEER, 128.

at their prayers and intervention God would receive our petition," hence demonstrating that already in the fourth century reference to the intercessory prayer of the saints such as we see in EgBAS and APsyr is appearing in eucharistic euchology. Indeed, the addition of the *Theotokos* to *Mystagogical Catechesis* 5.9 would give us something remarkably similar to the commemoration in EgBAS.

While we must be somewhat cautious about the possibility of *liturgical* evidence in the early eucharistic prayers for the use of the term *Theotokos*, at least more so outside of Egypt, the fifth-century Byzantine historian Socrates provides the following information about Origen of Alexandria:

> Origen . . . in the first volume of his *Commentaries* on the apostle's epistle to the Romans, gives an ample exposition of the sense in which the term *Theotokos* is used. It is therefore obvious that Nestorius had very little acquaintance with the treatises of the ancients, and for that reason . . . objected to the word only; for that he does not assert Christ to be a mere man, as Photinus did or Paul of Samosata, his own published homilies fully demonstrate.[23]

Unfortunately, the Greek text of Origen's *Commentary on Romans* is lost and Rufinus's Latin translation omits any reference to the term in the section of chapter 1 where it may once have been present. In her recent critical edition of this commentary, however, Caroline P. Hammond Bammel does indicate in the notes where the term may have occurred in the Greek text, as part of Origen's comments on the description of Paul in 1.3–4 of Christ being both the Son of God and son of David in the flesh.[24]

Apart from Socrates, there are other references to *Theotokos* in at least two fragments of Origen's writings that do tend to be considered authentic. According to the TLG, there are three occurrences of the term in *Fragmenta in Lucam* (not surprisingly, all in the context of Luke 2) and one appearance in *Selecta in Deuteronomium*. In other words, there are, including Socrates' text, as many as *five* possible references to the *Theotokos* in Origen's writings. And, as Starowieyski notes,

[23] NPNF, 2, 2nd series, 171.
[24] Caroline P. Hammond Bammel, *Der Römerbriefkommentar des Origenes: Kritische Ausgabe der Übersetzung Rufins, Buch 1–3* (Freiburg: Verlag Herder, 1990), 56.

while theologians often contest this "evidence," patristic scholars generally accept it![25]

At least from the first quarter of the fourth century on, then, the term *Theotokos* rapidly became a common title for the Virgin Mary that cut across both ecclesial lines as well as the boundaries of what might be called orthodoxy and heresy. While the term itself is hard to document before the third century, a growing mariological interest was certainly fostered by Justin Martyr and Irenaeus of Lyons in their theology of Mary as the "New Eve"[26] as well as by marian narratives, like the mid-second- to early third-century *Protoevangelium of James*. Hence, it would not be surprising at all to find this title in some third-century theological discourse. Indeed, the fact that fourth-century patristic authors of such diverse christological positions can equally employ the term does strongly suggest a common, earlier, and shared history of the term.

Some recent scholarship on the acceptance of the title *Theotokos* at Ephesus occasionally suggests that the term itself is one that was both liturgical and devotional in use, without going into much detail as to how this might have been the case.[27] We have seen that there is no undisputed evidence for its appearance in liturgical usage, although it seems that in some places like Egypt the appearance of the *Theotokos* in eucharistic praying would not be out of the ordinary. It remains to be seen, however, if it was devotional in nature, that is, rooted in popular piety. But in saying this, it must be remembered, as we saw in the previous chapter, that early Christians did not make the same kinds of distinctions between "official" and "popular" religion or piety that modern scholars have tended to make. Nor can we say, especially with regard to devotion to Mary and the saints that it was some kind of lower-class form of "worship" for the uneducated

---

[25] Starowieyski, "Le titre Θεοτόκος," 237. "Ce témoignage contesté souvent par le théologiens, est généralement accepté par les patroloques."

[26] On Mary as the "New Eve," see Pelikan, *Mary through the Centuries*, 39–52.

[27] See the critical approaches of Richard Price, "Theotokos: The Title and Its Significance in Doctrine and Devotion," in Boss, *Mary: The Complete Resource*, 56–74, and Stephen J. Shoemaker, "Marian Liturgies and Devotion in Early Christianity," in Boss, *Mary: The Complete Resource*, 130–45. See also Stephen Shoemaker, "The Cult of the Virgin in the Fourth Century: A Fresh Look at Some Old and New Sources," in Maunder, *The Origins of the Cult of the Virgin Mary*, 71–88.

masses. In this context, bishop, theologian, emperor, and the members of the faithful shared a common relationship of devotion, albeit perhaps with different ends or goals in view.[28]

In an article several years ago, Cyrille Vogel[29] noted that until the middle of the second century ancient burial inscriptions reveal that Christians prayed both *for* and *to* deceased Christians, whether they were martyrs or not, a point underscored by Taft in a recent essay as well.[30] Such prayer *for* deceased baptized Christians as part of the *communio sanctorum*, of course, is highly consistent with CHR, where, as we have seen, prayer is made *for* (ὑπὲρ) the *Theotokos* and the saints, and ArmBAS, where the *Theotokos* and the saints are simply commemorated at the Eucharist.[31] One might also note that the Roman *canon missae* is rather striking in this regard since in its *Communicantes* the assembly merely prays in "communion" with and "venerates the memory" (*et memoriam venerantes*) of Mary, called *Genetrícis Dei et Dómini nostri Jesu Christi* ("Bearer or Mother of our God and Savior Jesus Christ"), and the saints and in the *Nobis quoque peccatoribus* merely asks for our admission into the company of the apostles and martyrs.

At the same time, by the end of the second century, prayer to or, at least, asking the martyrs in particular for their intercession, even with regard to their exercising the office of the keys, was becoming a rather common Christian practice.[32] Similarly, in *De Oratione* Origen himself not only witnesses to but actually advocates prayer to the saints, saying:

[28] In addition to 27–28 above, see also *A People's History of Christianity*, vol. 2: *Late Ancient Christianity*, ed. Virginia Burrus (Minneapolis: Fortress Press, 2005), 165–87, 188–210.

[29] Cyrille Vogel, "Priére ou intercession? Une ambiguïté dans le culte paléo-chrétien des martyrs," in *Communio Sanctorum: Mélanges offerts á Jean-Jacques von Allmen* (Geneva: Labor et Fides, 1982): 284–89.

[30] Taft, "Prayer to or for the Saints?," 439–55. See also Michael Kunzler, "Insbesondere für unsere allheilige Herrin . . . ," in *Gratias Agamus: Studien zum eucharistischen Hochgebet*, ed. A. Heinz and H. Rennings (Freiburg/Basel/Wien: Herder, 1992), 227–40.

[31] See above, note 13.

[32] See Frederick C. Klawiter, "The Role of Martyrdom and Persecution in Developing the Priestly Authority of Women in Early Christianity: A Case Study of Montanism," *Church History* 49, no. 3 (1980): 258–59; and Peter Brown, *The Cult of the Saints: Its Rise and Function in Latin Christianity* (Chicago: University of Chicago Press, 1981).

[I]t is not foolish to offer supplication, intercession, and thanksgiving also to the saints. Moreover, two of them, I mean intercession and thanksgiving, may be addressed not only to the saints but also to other people, while supplication may be addressed only to the saints if someone is found to be a Paul or a Peter so as to help us by making us worthy of receiving the authority given them to forgive sins.[33]

And, the fragmentary prayer called the Strasbourg Papyrus, quite possibly a complete eucharistic prayer, sometimes dated as early as second-century Egypt, already contains the following invocation: "grant us to have a part and lot with the fair . . . of your holy prophets, apostles, and martyrs. Receive(?) [through] their entreaties [these prayers]."[34]

It is also in the same third-century context of Origen, and Egyptian Christianity in general, where scholars have often dated the famous short marian prayer, usually called by its Latin title, *Sub tuum praesidium*, and translated as:

To your protection we flee, holy Mother of God (*Theotokos*):
do not despise our prayers in [our] needs,
but deliver us from all dangers,
glorious and blessed Virgin.[35]

Used liturgically in the Coptic, Greek, and Ambrosian Rites (for which the evidence is no earlier than the fifth and sixth century) and in the Roman Rite (for which evidence is no earlier than the seventh), the somewhat corrupted Greek version of this text in the manuscript published by C. H. Roberts in 1938 has been viewed as third century or even earlier.[36] Arguments against a third-century date tend to focus on the presence of the term *Theotokos* and reflect what may well be an example of a rather circular reasoning that since the term must be later, the text, therefore, cannot be earlier. But even if the text of

[33] Origen, *De Oratione* 14.6; ET from *Origen: An Exhortation to Martyrdom, Prayer, and Selected Works*, trans. Rowan A. Greer, The Classics of Western Spirituality (New York: Paulist Press, 1979), 111–12.

[34] PEER, 54.

[35] Translation from the Latin by Kilian McDonnell, "The Marian Liturgical Tradition," in Maxwell E. Johnson, ed., *Between Memory and Hope; Readings on the Liturgical Year* (Collegeville, MN: Liturgical Press, Pueblo, 2000), 387.

[36] See ibid. See also P. Feuillen Mercenier, "La plus ancienne prière à la Sain Vierge: le *Sub tuum praesidium*," *Les Questions Liturgiques et Paroissiales* 25 (1940): 33–36.

the *Sub tuum praesidium* is no older than the early *fourth* century, it remains the earliest marian prayer in existence—unless the greetings to Mary by the angel and Elizabeth (Luke 1) are already Christian hymn or devotional texts themselves—and testifies at least to some kind of marian devotional piety well before Ephesus! Indeed, it was already in the middle of the fourth century that Emperor Julian the Apostate in his *Against the Galileans* criticized "the superstition of Christians for invoking the Theotokos!"[37]

At the same time, there is nothing in this prayer of supplication to the *Theotokos* that would be inconsistent with Origen's own advocating of prayer to the saints or with his quite possible use of the title *Theotokos* in the third century. There is also nothing really inconsistent here between this *Sub tuum praesidium* prayer and the commemoration or intercession of the *Theotokos* in EgBAS or ArmBAS.

We should also take more into account the possible shaping of early marian devotional and liturgical piety by the mid-second- to early third-century *Protoevangelium of James*, which, as Robert Eno notes, is "unusual in that it showed some interest in and development on Mary for her own sake."[38] This apocryphal gospel, termed doctrinally "orthodox" by George Tavard:[39]

(1) gives us the names of Mary's parents, Joachim and Anna;

(2) defends Mary's *virginitas in partu* and even *post partum* in rather graphic detail;[40]

[37] As quoted in Pelikan, *Mary through the Centuries*, 56.

[38] Robert Eno, "Mary and Her Role in Patristic Theology," in *The One Mediator, the Saints, and Mary: Lutherans and Catholics in Dialogue 7*, ed. H. George Anderson et al. (Minneapolis, MN: Augsburg Fortress, 1992), 164. See also Chris Maunder, "Mary in the New Testament and Apocrypha," in Boss, *Mary: The Complete Resource*, 11–49; and J. K. Elliot, "Mary in the Apocryphal New Testament," in Maunder, *The Origins of the Cult of the Virgin Mary*, 57–70.

[39] George Tavard, *The Thousand Faces of the Virgin Mary* (Collegeville, MN: Liturgical Press, Michael Glazier, 1996), 19. On the influence of the apocryphal gospels on marian piety and iconography, see Ioannis Karavidopoulos, "On the Information Concerning the Virgin Mary Contained in the Apocryphal Gospels," in *Mother of God: Representations of the Virgin in Byzantine Art*, ed. Maria Vassilaki (Milan: Skira editore, 2000), 67–89.

[40] See below, 86f.

(3) provides us with the narrative contents of what will become two marian feasts later in the Christian East and West, i.e., her Nativity on September 8, and, when she was three-years old, her Presentation in the Temple on November 21;

(4) associates her closely with the Jerusalem Temple, and describes her as a "weaver" of the purple and scarlet for the temple veil, both images which, according to Nicholas Constas, will have a great influence on the marian theology of Proclus of Constantinople in the fifth-century controversy with Nestorius.[41] Indeed, the Virgin Mary as the "Ark" or "Tabernacle" in which the Logos made flesh dwells will be well attested in later Greek patristic literature.

And all of this is already in place—at least in this text—by the end of the second or beginning of the third century! That this narrative somehow remained dormant for two or three centuries and then, all of a sudden, is "discovered" and starts suggesting marian feasts, imagery, and theology seems rather unlikely.

But whatever one might conclude about marian devotional piety in the first three centuries, certainly by the middle of the fourth century liturgical prayers, hymns, and other texts illustrate that such devotion, and not only the title *Theotokos*, was becoming rather widespread. Together with Julian the Apostate's fourth-century charge of "superstition" against Christian prayer based on Christian invocations of the *Theotokos*, it is clear that some kind of poetic devotion is present also in mid-fourth-century Syria, especially in the hymns of Ephrem (d. 373 CE), which leads Sebastian Brock to conclude:

> In actual fact, the Christological differences that separate the Syrian Orthodox, Greek Orthodox (Chalcedonian) Churches and the Church of the East do not appear to have had much effect on their attitudes to Mary. . . . Thus those who are familiar with the Byzantine tradition will find much of what Syriac writers say on the subject of Mary not unfamiliar.[42]

---

[41] Constas, "Weaving the Body of God," 169–94.

[42] Sebastian Brock, "Mary in Syriac Tradition," in *Mary's Place in Christian Dialogue*, ed. A. Stacpoole (Wilton, CT: Morehouse-Barlow, 1982), 183.

And developing marian devotion and theology certainly has a place at the same time in Cappadocia, where Gregory Nazianzen has no qualms about declaring that "if anyone does not agree that Holy Mary is the Mother of God [ἐπὶ τῆς θεοτόκον τὴν ἁγίαν Μαρίαν], he is at odds with the Godhead."[43] It is also Nazianzen who in his *Oratio XXIV*, in a story about Cyprian of Antioch and the virgin Justina, refers to a prayer of intercession offered by Justina to "the Virgin Mary, imploring her to help a virgin in danger."[44] Similarly, Gregory of Nyssa in his treatise on virginity writes that:

> [Death] found at last in virginity a barrier beyond which he could not pass. Just as in the time of Mary, the Mother of God [ἐπὶ τῆς θεοτό κου Μαρίας], the Death who had reigned from Adam until then found, when he came to her and dashed his forces against the fruit of her virginity as against a rock, that he was himself shattered against her.[45]

And, of special interest in a devotional context, it is in his *Vita Gregorii thaumaturgi* where Nyssa refers to an apparition of both Mary ("the mother of the Lord") and the apostle John to Gregory the Wonder-worker, thereby providing the first reference to a marian apparition in the history of the church.[46] If, of course, neither of the above references to a prayer of intercession (Nazianzen) or to an apparition of Mary (Nyssa) tells us anything about the third-century context, they do "tell us . . . about the situation in the time of the writers."[47] And, for developing marian devotional piety that is what is significant.

---

[43] "Letter to Cledonius the Priest, against Apollinaris," in *Lettres Théologiques*, SC 208 (Paris: Éditions du Cerf, 1974); ET from William A. Jurgens, *The Faith of the Early Fathers*, vol. 2 (Collegeville, MN: Liturgical Press, 1979), 40–41.

[44] PG 35:1181ᵃ. ET from H. Graef, *Mary: A History of Doctrine and Devotion*, vol. 1 (New York: Sheed & Ward, 1963), 64.

[45] Jurgens, *The Faith of the Early Fathers*, vol. 2, 44.

[46] See PG 46:912. Such would explain why the TLG provides some nine references to a homily on the incarnation by Gregory the Wonderworker. This attribution, however, is not regarded as correct. See M. Jugie, "Les Homélies Mariales attribuées a Saint Grégoire le Thamaturge," *Analecta Bollandiana* 43 (1925): 86–95. At the same time, Jugie believed the vision itself to be authentic.

[47] Eno, "Mary and Her Role in Patristic Theology," 166.

That "there was a popular veneration for the Virgin Mother which threatened to run extravagant lengths"[48] in the fourth century is testified to by the *Panarion* of Epiphanius of Salamis (315–403 CE). According to his witness, not only was there in existence an anti-marian group called the *Antidicomarianites*, who denied Mary's perpetual virginity,[49] but also an extreme pro-marian group, known as the *Collyridians* (from κολλυρίς, "cakes"), a group comprised mostly of women who worshiped Mary as a "goddess," offered her and then consumed small cakes, and had a female priesthood. Epiphanius' critique of the *Collyridians*, while certainly warning against excessive marian piety, tends to be more about the subordinate role he believed that women should aspire to in the church in imitation of the passivity of Mary. Nevertheless, if he is a credible witness here, we not only see *some* developing marian popular piety in the time period of the fourth century but see that it was even prevalent enough to become problematic and heretical. As such, already in the fourth century we have some corroborating evidence for the statement of E. Ann Matter that "the practice of the pious often takes its own course,"[50] a maxim that will be demonstrated over and over again especially in the later history of marian doctrine and devotion, even unto our own day.

The best example of a popular marian piety, however, comes in early fifth-century Constantinople on the very eve of the controversy with Nestorius and the resulting Council of Ephesus. In his studies of the theology of Proclus of Constantinople, Nicholas Constas refers us to the following event, which took place shortly after Nestorius had become Patriarch of Constantinople:

> Nestorius was scandalized by the devotion to the Virgin which he encountered upon his arrival in Constantinople. Nestorius was further outraged to learn that during the reign of his predecessor the empress Pulcheria [whose spiritual advisor, in fact, had become Proclus] had

---

[48] Herbert Thurston, "Devotion to the Blessed Virgin Mary down to the Council of Nicaea," *The Catholic Encyclopedia*, vol. 15 (New York: Robert Appleton, 1914), online version: http://www.catholicity.com/encyclopedia/v/virgin_mary,devotion_to_bl.html.

[49] *Panarion* 79. Augustine himself (*De haeresibus* 56), based on Epiphanius, also refers to this group but *not* to the *Collyridians*.

[50] As quoted in Johnson, *Truly Our Sister*, 119.

been permitted to receive communion within the sanctuary of the Great Church. According to one source, Nestorius, barring the empress from the chancel screen, insisted that "Only priests may walk here," to which she replied, "Why, have I not given birth to God?" "You?" he retorted, "have given birth to Satan," and proceeded to drive Pulcheria from the sanctuary. Not long after this confrontation, Nestorius publicly challenged the dignity of the Virgin Mary and began to preach against the propriety of calling her the Theotokos—the Birth-giver of God. . . . The people of Constantinople, who are said to have been passionately devoted to theological discussion, were greatly offended at this. Besides, the term had been generally accepted by the bishops of the capital from at least the time of Gregory the Theologian. Unlike the term "homoousious" . . . the title "Theotokos" was a powerfully evocative word which belonged to the language of liturgy and devotion. As a result, local resistance to Nestorius formed quickly and was actively supported, and to a certain extent orchestrated by Proclus and Pulcheria.[51]

As this event certainly demonstrates, the ultimate dogmatic decision at Ephesus of Mary as *Theotokos* was rooted not simply in the theology of the unitive personhood of Christ but was also, undoubtedly, the product both of the *lex orandi* and popular piety and devotion. As far back as 1940, P. F. Mercenier had argued:

> In defending himself against Nestorius with a relentlessness, one might say, St. Cyril does not battle only with an opinion or a scholarly word, but with an expression and a belief consecrated for a long time by liturgical usage. . . . This would be a new application of the adage: *Legem credendi statuat lex supplicandi.*[52]

Indeed, consistent with the marian theology of Nestorius' predecessor, Atticus of Constantinople (d. 425), who had instructed Pulcheria and her sisters, Arcadia and Marina, that if they imitated the virginity and chastity of Mary, they would give birth to God mystically in their souls,[53] Pulcheria's marian self-identification ("Have I not given birth

---

[51] Constas, "Weaving the Body of God," 173–75. See also idem, *Proclus of Constantinople and the Cult of the Virgin in Late Antiquity: Homilies 1–5*, Supplements to Vigiliae Christiane LXVI (Leiden/Boston: Brill, 2003).

[52] Mercenier, "Le plus ancienne prière," 36.

[53] See Constas, "Weaving the Body of God," 171–72.

to God?") indicates that such personal or popular devotion to the *Theotokos* could even become a kind of marian mysticism.

Liturgical feasts are also important for how liturgy might be said to shape doctrine, and, hence, the context of Proclus and Nestorius is also important in this regard since the first two words of Proclus' famous homily delivered at the Great Church of Constantinople in the presence of Nestorius, probably in the year 430 CE, makes reference to "the Virgin's festival" being celebrated that day (παρθενικὴ πανήγυρις).[54] While it is somewhat unclear which marian feast is intended by Proclus' reference (the Annunciation, the Sunday before, and the Sunday after Christmas have all been suggested), current scholarship concludes that the feast in question was probably the day after Christmas, December 26, 430, "a day on which the Byzantine Church continued to celebrate a 'synaxis' in honor of the Theotokos."[55] In two places in his writings Athanasius refers to the necessity of keeping a "memory" or "commemoration" (μνήμη) of Mary.[56] Because of this, Jaroslav Pelikan, in line with Martin Jugié[57] and Hilda Graef,[58] who both underscored the pre-Ephesine existence of a marian "feast" on either the Sunday before or after Christmas in the East, has suggested "that evidence and his language seem to make it plausible that such a commemoration of Mary was being kept already during his time and that his argument was based on it."[59] Such would make this marian feast already associated with Christmas a mid-fourth-century reality, although it cannot be ruled out that Athanasius may simply be referring to the memory of Mary or, perhaps, even to the type of anaphoral commemoration we have noted above.

That the Virgin Mary ultimately should come to be commemorated liturgically in relationship to the feast of Christmas in both East and West is surely no surprise. But apart from Athanasius' use of μνήμη there is simply no clear evidence of such a feast prior to Proclus' homily, and it is quite possible that this feast had been instituted

---

[54] Constas, *Proclus of Constantinople and the Cult of the Virgin in Late Antiquity*, 136.

[55] Ibid., 58.

[56] *Letter to Epictetus* 4 and *Letter to Maximus the Philosopher* 3.

[57] M. Jugie, "La première fête mariale en Orient et en Occident, l'Avent primitif," *Echos d'Orient* 26, no. 130 (1923): 129–52.

[58] Graef, *Mary: A History*, vol. 1, 133.

[59] Pelikan, *Mary through the Centuries*, 61.

at Constantinople no earlier than Atticus himself or Sisinnius (426–427).[60] But that *a* feast associated so closely with Christmas should already be known by Athanasius does not seem likely. Indeed, our first reference to Christmas itself being celebrated in the East is *Apostolic Constitutions* 8.33.6, usually dated today around 381 CE.[61]

This does not mean, however, that there was not *a* marian feast or commemoration in existence prior to the fifth century or that Athanasius himself could not have known of its existence and celebration at Alexandria. Indeed, the oldest marian feast in existence is usually identified as the August 15 celebration of Mary *Theotokos*, having its origins in Jerusalem and first documented in the fifth-century *Armenian Lectionary*, one of our major guides to liturgical life in late fourth-century Jerusalem. The entry in the *Armenian Lectionary*[62] reads:

> Com. MARY THEOTOKOS, at *Second Mile from Bethlehem*, 15 August
> PS + ANT: 132 (a8)
> O.T. LESSON: Isa. 7-10
> APOSTLE: Gal. 3.29–4.7
> ALL/PS: 110.1
> GOSPEL: Luke 2.1-7

Pierre Jounel summarizes the standard theory about this feast succinctly;

> The liturgical cult of Mary originated in Jerusalem, with the feast of August 15 as its foundation. Initially celebrated at the Kathisma or place where according to tradition Mary paused to rest before going on to Bethlehem, the feast was transferred, toward the end of the fifth century, to Gethsemane and the basilica where people venerated the tomb of the Virgin. The feast of Mary Theotokos thus became the feast of the Dormition of the Mother of God. At the end of the sixth

---

[60] See Constas, *Proclus of Constantinople and the Cult of the Virgin in Late Antiquity*, 58. See also Margot Fassler, "The First Marian Feast in Constantinople and Jerusalem: Chant Texts, Readings, and Homiletic Literature," in *The Study of Medieval Chant: Paths and Bridges, East and West; In Honor of Kenneth Levy*, ed. Peter Jeffrey (Rochester: Boydell Press, 2000), 29–42.

[61] See Marcel Metzger, *Les Constitutions Apostoliques*, 3, SC 336, 242–43.

[62] Text from A. Renoux, *Le Codex arménien Jérusalem 121*, Patrologia Orientalis 36/2 (Turnout: Brepols, 1971), 355–57. ET from John Wilkinson, *Egeria's Travels* (London: SPCK, 1971), 274.

century, Emperor Maurice ruled that this feast was to be celebrated throughout the empire.[63]

With regard to the August 15 date, however, various assumptions have been offered, including seeing August 15 as but the date of the Kathisma's dedication, or of Jerusalem deliberately distancing itself from Constantinople's Christmas-related marian feast since it held out longer before succumbing to the new December 25 date for the celebration of Christ's beginnings. More recent scholarship, reflected especially in the work of Walter Ray,[64] has argued that the August 15 feast is among the most primitive in the Jerusalem liturgical tradition and has its origins in an early Jerusalem commemoration of the incarnation or annunciation, nine months before a primitive celebration of Christ's nativity in May. In fact, the earliest station for the feast, as reflected in the *Armenian Lectionary*, two or three miles from Bethlehem, is already part of the narrative of Christ's birth in the *Protoevangelium of James*.[65] Hence, if Ray is correct, some kind of devotion, even liturgical, may have been part of the early Jerusalem tradition, and it may well be that if Athanasius has any feast in mind by his use of the word μνήμη it is this one.

Again, while it is not only liturgy that gives rise to the adoption of the title *Theotokos* at the Council of Ephesus, it is not suprising that the tradition where we find most of the early liturgical evidence for the title is the Egyptian from where, through Cyril of Alexandria, that title is strongly defended against Nestorius. With special reference to the hymn *Sub tuum praesidium*, Jaroslav Pelikan writes, "Here, too, theology had to come to terms with liturgy."[66] And, although we cannot know with certainty how far back a *lex orandi* with regard to

[63] P. Jounel, "The Veneration of Mary," in *The Church at Prayer*, vol. 4: *Liturgy and Time*, ed. A. G. Martimort et al. (Collegeville, MN: Liturgical Press, 1986), 131.

[64] Walter Ray, *August 15 and the Development of the Jerusalem Calendar* (PhD diss., University of Notre Dame, 2000). See also Stephen J. Shoemaker, *Ancient Traditions of the Virgin Mary's Dormition and Assumption* (New York: Oxford University Press, 2002).

[65] See Ray, *August 15*, 56ff.

[66] Jaroslav Pelikan, *The Christian Tradition: A History of the Development of Doctrine*, vol. 1: *The Emergence of the Catholic Tradition (100–600)* (Chicago: University of Chicago Press, 1971), 241.

Mary herself goes, it is quite clear that this was developing long before the controversies that brought about the Council of Ephesus itself.

3. The Council of Chalcedon and Liturgical Controversy

One of the unfortunate results of the Council of Ephesus was the split it caused within Eastern Christianity. Because that body of East Syrian Christians, still known today as the Ancient Church of the East, had adopted the Christology of Nestorius at the Synod of Seleucia-Ctesiphon (ca. 410), a split between this church and the rest of both Eastern and Western Christianity resulted after the Council of Ephesus and has remained so for centuries, with members of this ancient tradition often called in the past by the pejorative term, "Nestorian."[67] But, as we saw above, in spite of their rejection of the official title of Mary as *Theotokos*, Sebastian Brock notes that with regard to Mary herself very little differentiates the Church of the East from the rest of the Christian East.

For those churches that accepted the Council of Ephesus as Orthodox teaching, the next major controversy, of course, concerned the precise relationship between Christ's divinity and humanity. And here two positions developed along the lines of those who claimed that after the incarnation Christ had but one nature uniting humanity and divinity in himself, a position associated with the Alexandrian school and called either "Monophysite" or "Miaphysite," and those who claimed that after the incarnation Christ united two complete natures in himself, divine and human, a position associated with the Antiochene school and called "Diaphysite." Like the other three ecumenical councils considered in this study, the particular details and results of the Council of Chalcedon are readily available elsewhere.[68] Here we need only note the end result, suggested by the *Tomus Ad Flavianum* (Letter to the Emperor Flavian) from Pope Leo I, often

---

[67] See Sebastian Brock, "The 'Nestorian' Church: A Lamentable Misnomer," in idem, *Fire from Heaven: Studies in Syriac Theology and Liturgy* (Aldershot/Burlington: Ashgate, 2006), 1–14.

[68] In addition to Pelikan, *The Christian Tradition*, vol. 1, 256ff., see Jenkins, *The Jesus Wars*, 199–226. For several primary texts in translation, see Richard A. Norris Jr., *The Christological Controversy* (Philadelphia: Fortress Press, 1980), 123ff.

called Leo's Tome, which was read and accepted at the council. As a result, the following Chalcedonian formula was adopted:

> Following, then, the holy fathers, we unite in teaching all to confess the one and only Son, our Lord Jesus Christ. This self-same one is perfect [*teleion*] both in deity [*theoteti*] and also in human-ness [*anthropoteti*]; this self-same one is also actually [*alethos*] God and actually man, with a rational soul [*psyches logikes*] and a body. He is of the same reality as the Father [*homousion to patri*] as far as his deity is concerned and of the same reality as we are ourselves [*homoousion hemin*] as far as his human-ness is concerned; thus like us in all respects, sin only excepted. Before time began [*pro ainonion*] he was begotten of the Father, in respect of his deity, and now in these "last days," for us and for our salvation, this selfsame one was born of Mary the virgin, who is God-bearer [*theotokos*] in respect of his human-ness [*anthropoteta*]. [We also teach] that we apprehend [*gnoridzomenon*] this one and only Christ-Son, Lord, only-begotten-in two natures [*duo phsesin*]; [and we do this] without confusing the two natures [*asunkutos*], without transmuting one nature into the other [*atreptos*], without dividing them into two separate categories [*adiairetos*], without contrasting them according to area or function [*achoristos*]. The distinctiveness of each nature is not nullified by the union. Instead, the "properties" [*idiotetos*] of each nature are conserved and both natures concur [*suntrechouses*] in one "person" [*prosopon*] and in one *hypostasis*. They are not divided or cut into two *prosopa*, but are together the one and only-begotten Logos of God, the Lord Jesus Christ. Thus have the prophets of old testified; thus the Lord Jesus Christ himself taught us; thus the Synod of the Fathers [Nicea] has handed down [*paradedoke*] to us.[69]

Like the Council of Ephesus, Chalcedon also resulted in another tragic split within the Christian East with the churches in support of the Miaphysite or Alexandrian position essentially cut off from communion with those who accepted Chalcedon as orthodox. What this has meant ever since is that, along with the earlier division in Christianity after Ephesus, now the Christian world is divided along the lines of "Chalcedonian" and "non-Chalcedonian" churches, the latter

---

[69] Translation adapted from *Creeds of the Churches: A Reader in Christian Doctrine from the Bible to the Present*, trans. John H. Leith, 3rd ed. (Louisville: Westminster/John Knox Press, 1982), 35–36.

of which have been often perjoratively called "Monophysite." The non-Chalcedonian churches include the Armenian Apostolic Church, the Coptic Orthodox Church, the Ethiopian Orthodox Church, and what became known as the Syrian Orthodox Church, reflecting an Antiochene or West Syrian tradition rather than East Syrian. As Ephrem Carr explains:

> Syrian Christians became divided by reason of the council of Chalcedon [451] into Melkites, who were loyal to the council and the emperor (*malko* = "ruler" or "king"), and the anti-chalcedonians. The Melkites gradually accepted also the liturgy of the imperial capital and became by the twelfth century part of the Byzantine rite. The Syrian faithful who rejected the council slowly formed their own church, a move fostered by Jacob Baradai (+ 578) and his establishment of an independent hierarchy from 543 onward. Thus the Syrian church came to be called Jacobite.[70]

Unlike the first three councils, it is difficult to apply a *lex orandi, lex credendi* argument to the development of the Chalcedonian decree on Christ's two natures. That is, it does not appear that liturgical texts or practices were involved in shaping what became known as the "hypostatic union," namely, that two complete natures are held together by a personal union. Nevertheless, as Pelikan writes, "the locus of the controversy, as could have been expected, was in the liturgy. If it was liturgically traditional and dogmatically proper to call Mary Theotokos and by this title to predicate birth of the Second Person of the Trinity, the suffering of the cross could also be legitimately attributed to him."[71]

The liturgical locus in this particular context was the entrance hymn incorporated into the liturgy of Constantinople during the Patriarchate of Proclus, namely, the *Trisagion*: "Holy God, Holy Mighty One, Holy Immortal One, have mercy on us!"[72] Originally interpreted

---

[70] Ephrem Carr, "Liturgical Families in the East," in *Handbook for Liturgical Studies*, vol. 1: *Introduction to the Liturgy*, ed. Anscar J. Chupungco (Collegeville, MN: Liturgical Press, Pueblo, 1997), 11–24, here at 15.

[71] Pelikan, *The Christian Tradition*, vol. 1, 270.

[72] On the *Trisagion* in addition to ibid., 91–110, see Sebastià Janeras, "Les byzantins et le *trisagion* christologique," in *Miscellanea liturgica in onore di Sua Eminenza*

christologically, this hymn came to be used not only in the emerging Byzantine Eucharistic Rite in Constantinople but also in the several developing rites elsewhere in the East, Chalcedonian and non-Chalcedonian alike. The non-Chalcedonians, however, before the petition for mercy, added to the text and have kept the relative clause, "Who was crucified for us." This was, in fact, added first by Patriarch Peter the Fuller at Antioch in 468,[73] who had actually taught his pet parrot to sing the *Trisagion* with this additional clause attached. Since in the developing Byzantine Rite the *Trisagion* was interpreted as a *trinitarian* hymn, what came to be regarded as the "Theopaschite" (suffering of God) clause was viewed and rejected not only as an innovation within the now rather common liturgical tradition but as a heretical (Monophysite) insertion suggesting that it was the Trinity itself that was incarnated, suffered, and died. Nevertheless, if this clause was an addtion or innovation in the *Trisagion*, it did underscore its original christological interpretation. And, by drawing attention to the belief that the Second Person of the Trinity did, indeed, suffer in the flesh upon the cross, the very question is raised even for the worship of the Person of Christ with regard to what is meant by the Chalcedonian formula when it says: "The 'properties' [*idiotetos*] of each nature are conserved and both natures concur [*suntrechouses*] in one 'person' [*prosopon*] and in one *hypostasis*. They are not divided or cut into two *prosopa*, but are together the one and only-begotten Logos of God, the Lord Jesus Christ." This christological principle of what is called the *communicatio idiomatum*, the communion of properties of each nature, was, notes Pelikan:

> responsible for the debate over the title Theotokos, and over the phrase "one of the Trinity suffered in the flesh," for it affirmed the propriety of ascribing to the total person of the God-man actions and

---

il Cardinale Giacomo Lercaro, vol. 2 (Rome: Desclée, 1967), 469–99; and idem, "Le trisagion : Une formule brève en liturgie comparée," in *Comparative Liturgy Fifty Years after Anton Baumstark (1872–1948)*, ed. Robert F. Taft and Gabriele Winkler, Orientalia Christiana Analecta 265 (Rome: Pontificio Istituto Orientale, 2002), 495–562.

[73] See the discussion of this in Hans-Joachim Schulz, *The Byzantine Liturgy* (Collegeville, MN: Liturgical Press, Pueblo, 1986), 22–25; and see the work of Janeras in note 72 above.

attributes of his humanity. But it also moved in the opposite direc-
tion. Worship was appropriately addressed to the total person of the
God-man, too, not only to his divinity, for by the communication of
properties the entire person was worthy of adoration.[74]

And probably nothing better illustrates this adoration of the entire
person of the God-Man liturgically than the following hymn, *O Monogenes* (Only Begotten), incorporated into the eucharistic liturgy of
Constantinople during the reign of Emperor Justinian I (527–565 CE):

> Only-Begotten Son and Word of God, immortal as you are,
>> You condescended for our salvation to be incarnate
>> from the Holy Theotokos and ever-virgin Mary,
>> and without undergoing change, You became Man;
> You were crucified O Christ God, and you trampled death by your
>> death;
>> You are One of the Holy Trinity;
>> equal in glory with the Father and the Holy Spirit:
>> save us![75]

This liturgical chant, now appearing within the entrance rites of the
Byzantine liturgy rather accurately summarizes the doctrinal conclusions of the councils of Nicea, Constantinople, Ephesus, and quite
possibly Chalcedon. It must be noted, however, that while this hymn
was added to the liturgy in Constantinople by those who accepted the
Council of Chalcedon, the mere fact that the non-Chalcedonian Armenian Apostolic Church also incorporated this into their eucharistic
liturgy mitigates against seeing it as reflecting only a Chalcedonian
interpretation of the Person of Christ.

4. Conclusion

If the question of the relationship between worship and doctrine,
praying shaping believing, is not as clear in the case of the further
development of christological doctrine at the councils of Ephesus
and Chalcedon as it was for Nicea and Constantinople, there is no

[74] Pelikan, *The Christian Tradition*, vol. 1, 271–72.
[75] For the Greek text, see LEW, 365–66.

question but that it does continue to play some formative role even here. As we have seen, especially in the first part of this chapter, the title of *Theotokos*, while, of course, christological in a broad sense, appears as a more general honorific title for Mary among diverse fourth-century authors with diverse christological positions! In other words, *Theotokos* as a title for Mary does not appear to be tied originally to a *particular* christological position as a banner of orthodoxy as it will come to be at and after the Council of Ephesus. Prior to that, it is simply one honorific way in which to refer to Mary.

Liturgically as well, the use of the title *Theotokos* itself, including our earliest marian hymn or prayer, the *Sub tuum praesidium*, may well be mid-third-century Alexandrian in origins. Origen himself, as testified to by Socrates, may well have been the first to have used this title in theological discourse, and the developing anaphoral tradition appears to be consistent with the growing development of prayer and supplication to the saints, as testified to in general by the cult of the martyrs and by Origen in particular. Already by the end of the second century, the *Protoevangelium of James* reflects an interest in Mary herself and provides several marian elements that will develop further and become, ultimately, the content of theological reflection, liturgical festal celebration, and popular devotion to her in the life of the church, with the earliest marian feast on August 15, quite possibly being a commemoration of Jesus' conception within the earliest days of Christianity itself. Hence, even the "christological" doctrinal controversy with Nestorius of Constantinople is not merely about doctrine. Rather, in the context of the late fourth and early fifth centuries, where marian devotion is witnessed to not only in Egypt but in Cappadocia (Gregory of Nyssa and Gregory Nazianzen) and Syria (Ephrem) as well, the controversy is also liturgical-devotional, as certainly indicated by what might be called the "marian mysticism" of Atticus, Pulcheria, and Proclus.

In such a multifaceted way, then, does the Virgin Mary, as *Theotokos*, become the very doctrinal and liturgical safeguard of the identity and personhood of Christ as the God-Man for what is recognized as orthodox Christian theology. Or, to say that another way, even if Mariology is but an implicate of Christology, generally speaking, it is this orthodox Mariology that keeps Christology "Orthodox." And, it is worth noting that it is especially within those liturgical traditions in both East and West, where marian feasts, commemorations, prayers, and devotions exist in abundance, that, officially at least, such a high or Orthodox Christology tends to be maintained.

With regard to the role of liturgy at Chalcedon, as we have seen, very little can be said. Even here, however, importance of the liturgy is certainly present, at least contextually, with the interpretation of hymns such as the *Trisagion* and, later, with the *O Monogenes* in the developing Eastern rites. If the formative role of praying is not as certain with Chalcedon, there is no question but that praying and believing are still held together within an Orthodox synthesis. If it is not so clear that the *lex orandi* leads to a *lex credendi* at Chalcedon, it is still the case, as Jaroslav Pelikan was quoted above, that the "locus of the controversy . . . was in the liturgy!" Praying and believing go together.

Chapter 4

Worship and Praxis

So far in this study we have been concerned with the relationship of praying and believing, with the role of liturgy in the formation and development of doctrine in early Christianity. To this must be added now another element, namely, *praxis*, or *orthopraxis*, i.e., whether or not worship also forms the ethical and moral praxis of the church and of individual Christians in the world and, if so, how it did this in the ancient Christian world. In his recent study, *Meeting Mystery*, Nathan Mitchell calls for what he terms the "verification" of Christian worship in the "liturgy of the neighbor," writing:

> Christian ritual is best understood as tablature or musical score—and that liturgical scores are "rhizomal, nomadic," limitlessly multiple in meaning and internally "indeterminate," that is, capable of verification only through the *exteriority* of ethical action. Christian liturgy begins as ritual practice but ends as ethical performance. Liturgy of the neighbor verifies liturgy of the church, much as a composer's score makes *music* only through the risk of performance. . . .
>
> . . . The slogan *lex orandi, lex credendi* does not, then, offer as much light as it may seem to promise. In spite of the tension between them, doxology and doctrine remain a cozy *ménage à deux*, each partner in the pair defining itself in terms of the other. But the deeper question is not whether faith controls worship, or vice versa, but whether either of them can be verified in the absence of a *lex agendi* (a rule of action or behavior), an ethical imperative that flows from the Christian's encounter with a God who is radically "un-God-like," a God who, in the cross of Jesus and in the bodies of the "poor, the hungry, the thirsty, the naked, the imprisoned," has become everything we believe a God is *not*. The ethical imperative implied by the phrase *lex agendi* breaks apart our comfortable "faith and worship" duo by introducing that subversive element of *indeterminacy*.[1]

---

[1] Nathan Mitchell, *Meeting Mystery: Liturgy, Worship, and Sacraments* (Maryknoll, NY: Orbis Books, 2006), 38–40, 223–25.

Elsewhere, he underscores this "ethical imperative" in relationship to his definition of liturgy as "God's work" for us, not "our work" for God:

> Liturgy is God's work for us, not our work for God. Only God can show us how to worship God—fittingly, beautifully. Liturgy is not something beautiful *we* do for God, but something beautiful *God* does for us and among us. Public worship is neither our work nor our possession; as the *Rule of St. Benedict* reminds us, it is *opus Dei, God's* work. *Our* work is to feed the hungry, to refresh the thirsty, to clothe the naked, to care for the sick, to shelter the homeless; to visit the imprisoned; to welcome the stranger; to open our hands and hearts to the vulnerable and the needy. If we are doing those things well, liturgy and the Catholic identity it rehearses will very likely take care of themselves.[2]

And in his famous *Doxology*, Geoffrey Wainwright also called for what he termed a "test of ethical correspondence" to be applied to worship and doctrine as well.[3]

Several years ago Rodney Stark, in his groundbreaking sociological study of Christian origins, *The Rise of Christianity*, underscored how it was doctrine itself that serves as the best explanation for how the early Christian community acted and how Christianity was successful over and against Greco-Roman pagan culture. Doctrine, in fact, for him was the "*ultimate factor*" in explaining why it was that Christianity became the dominant religious force in the empire after Constantine:

> *Central doctrines of Christianity prompted and sustained attractive, liberating, and effective social relations and organizations.* I believe that it was the religion's particular doctrines that permitted Christianity to be among the most sweeping and successful revitalization movements in history. And it was the way these doctrines took on actual flesh, the way they directed organizational actions and individual behavior, that led to the rise of Christianity.[4]

[2] Nathan Mitchell, "The Amen Corner: Being Good and Being Beautiful," *Worship* 74, no. 6 (November 2000): 557–58.

[3] Geoffrey Wainwright, *Doxology: The Praise of God in Worship, Doctrine and Life* (New York: Oxford University Press, 1980), 245.

[4] Rodney Stark, *The Rise of Christianity: A Sociologist Reconsiders History* (Princeton, NJ: Princeton University Press, 1996), 211; emphasis is original.

In particular, he notes, "surely doctrine was central to nursing the sick during times of plague, to the rejection of abortion and infanticide, to fertility, and to organizational vigor."[5] Here, in Christianity, was the alternative to the lack of adequate health care in general; to the high mortality rate of women due to, among other things, the prevalence of abortions; to the decreased number of women of marrying age as the result of the infanticide of female babies; and to the overall violent nature (the gladiatorial "games") of the Greco-Roman pagan context. And the alternative was provided by Christian *praxis*, motivated by the God of love for all, whose grace and unconditional love they encountered regularly in worship.

Stark did not, however, deal with worship in his study. And, to his credit, it was not the liturgical life itself, of course, that attracted others to the Christian faith in the earlier periods of this development, and, hence, Christianity did not conquer because others were attracted to its public worship. Not until after Constantine did Christian liturgy move from its earlier domestic to a now public setting, becoming itself a *cultus publicus* made increasingly possible by imperial support. But worship certainly did play a role even in the earliest days, even if indirect. As noted previously in this study, Alan Kreider has drawn attention to the following characteristic of liturgy in early Christianity:

> Christian worship was designed to enable *Christians* to worship God. *It was not designed to attract non-Christians*; it was *not "seeker-sensitive."* For seekers were not allowed in. . . . Christian worship . . . assisted in the outreach of the churches indirectly, as a by-product, by shaping the lives and character of individual Christians and their communities so that they would be intriguing.[6]

If Stark's work can be interpreted as the vindication of doctrine and/or believing leading to ethics or moral action in early Christianity, the focus of this chapter is the relationship of worship itself to the "liturgy of the neighbor" or the "ethical imperative," to use Mitchell's categories. That is, is there in early Christianity something akin to a *lex agendi* (or *lex bene operandi*, "law of good working") that

---

[5] Ibid., 209.

[6] Alan Kreider, *The Change of Conversion and the Origin of Christendom* (Harrisburg, PA: Trinity Press International, 1999), 14; emphasis added.

does function as the verification or authenticator of both the *lex orandi* and the *lex credendi*? In order to attempt an answer to this complex question, this chapter will focus first on biblical texts, especially some key New Testament texts that appear to deal with the implications of worship in the ongoing life of the church. Second, homilies and other texts from the later patristic period will be investigated with regard to the further development of this presumed relationship in a time much different from that of the New Testament era. The overall thesis of this chapter is simple: Christians act morally or ethically because of what they believe, and what they believe is continually shaped by worship, by how they are formed by the words and acts of worship, by the divine encounter with the God of grace and love mediated in the liturgy via its spoken words, texts, acts, gestures, and sacramental signs. It is not the only place where this encounter happens, of course. But, as we have seen previously, it is, indeed, a privileged place.

1. *Lex Orandi, Lex Credendi, Lex Agendi* and the Bible

The relationship between worship and ethics, or what many today refer to as "liturgy and justice," is at least as old as the Hebrew prophets in the several centuries before Christ. And among those prophets it was the mid-eighth-century BCE prophet Amos who made the clearest statement about that relationship in the following text, a text that can also serve as a fitting summary of Amos' entire message:

> I hate, I despise your festivals,
>   and I take no delight in your solemn assemblies.
> Even though you offer me your burnt offerings and grain offerings,
>   I will not accept them;
> and the offerings of well-being of your fatted animals
>   I will not look upon.
> Take away from me the noise of your songs;
>   I will not listen to the melody of your harps.
> But let justice roll down like waters,
>   and righteousness like an ever-flowing stream. (Amos 5:21-24)

I often point to this text in my undergraduate courses in beginning theology as an example of "liturgical theology." God rejects Israel's worship not because it was done poorly or improperly but precisely because the connection between worship and life was not being made or sustained by the worshipers. In other words, the worship of God at mid-eighth-century Bethel and Dan was not being verified or authenticated by the ethical behavior of the people. Justice was being neglected and ignored even though these shrines were doing a booming business and the liturgical sacrifices, especially of the wealthy, were abundant.[7]

While other Old Testament prophetic texts could be presented underscoring the same basic theme (e.g., Isa 1:1–5:24 or Mic 3:1-12), similar descriptions of this relationship appear throughout the New Testament. In his recent book *The Four Gospels on Sunday*, Gordon Lathrop argues that the gospels themselves are explicitly concerned with what happens in, and are written for, the "liturgical" assemblies of the early Christian communities themselves. And here it is important to note that Christianity in its origins was indeed primarily a "meal fellowship." That is, as Lathrop writes, "the early Christian movement seems to have come into existence and to have continued to spread as a meal fellowship. At least recent historical scholarship has strongly urged this idea in a fairly wide consensus."[8] Hence, according to him, what we actually see in the gospel writers' addresses to these various meal fellowships are the origins of what becomes the Eucharist itself. Eucharistic "origins are being enacted before our eyes in these texts as we see that the diverse meal practices of first- and second-century Christianity were being brought under the apostolic and evangelical critique which called for these meals to show forth

---

[7] One of the best commentaries on Amos is still that of James Luther Mays, *Amos: A Commentary*, Old Testament Library (Philadelphia: Westminster/John Knox Press, 1969).

[8] Gordon Lathrop, *The Four Gospels on Sunday: The New Testament and the Reform of Christian Worship* (Minneapolis: Fortress Press, 2012), 40–41. On early Jewish, Christian, and Greco-Roman meal practices, see Blake Leyerle, "Meal Customs in the Greco-Roman World," in *Two Liturgical Traditions: Passover and Easter; Origin and History to Modern Times*, ed. Paul Bradshaw and Lawrence Hoffman (Notre Dame, IN: University of Notre Dame Press, 1999), 29–61; Andrew McGowan, *Ascetic Eucharists* (Oxford: Clarendon Press, 1999); and Paul F. Bradshaw and Maxwell E. Johnson, *The Eucharistic Liturgies: Their Evolution and Interpretation* (Collegeville, MN: Liturgical Press, Pueblo, 2012), 1–24.

the death of Jesus until he comes."[9] Therefore the evangelists themselves provide a word of critique and reform for those assemblies.
In Mark, that word spoken by his gospel is that the cross of the risen
one who remains the crucified one must be central in its meal sharing.
In Matthew, the focus is also on the cross but includes the reference
to "forgiveness of sins" associated with the eucharistic cup and calls
the Matthean meal fellowship to minister to the hungry, thirsty, sick,
naked, and imprisoned (Matt 25). In Luke, the meal characteristics
of the Last Supper and Emmaus accounts "are being urged by the
Gospel exactly so that the meal keeping with the churches may be the
meal with the widow [Luke 4:14-30], with Levi [Luke 5:27-38], and
with Zacchaeus [Luke 19:1-10], and may thus become the breaking
of the bread and distribution to the poor imaged in Acts 2:42-47."[10]
And in John, by means of the "bread of life" discourse (John 6:25-71)
and the washing of feet at the Last Supper (John 13), the Johannine
"meal fellowship" is called to recognize "the depth of their meals
as an encounter with the crucified one who gives himself away in
love."[11] In all of these cases, therefore, the meals of these fellowships
are to lead toward ministry either within the communities or outside
of those communities, ministries associated closely with feeding the
poor. If Lathrop is correct in his interpretation, it is precisely the relationship of worship, doctrine, and ethics that the gospels address.
Whatever theological interpretation of early Christian meals there
might have been before, certainly some sense of the ongoing presence of Christ within those meals called for greater doctrinal clari-
fication of that presence which was offered by the gospel writers
within the various narratives of the institution of that meal, at least
with regard to catechesis if not liturgical text. And the celebration
of those meals included this ethical imperative of love and mercy
toward others. While he does not use the words himself, Lathrop's
approach is clearly one of *lex orandi, lex credendi, lex agendi*, although,
as evangelical addresses offering words of critique and reform for
the "liturgies" of these communities, one might say that a priority is
given by him here to the *lex credendi* in shaping and reforming liturgical and ethical practice.

[9] Lathrop, *The Four Gospels on Sunday*, 55.
[10] Ibid., 48.
[11] Ibid., 53.

Our earliest New Testament account of the narrative of the institution of the Eucharist, 1 Corinthians 11:17-34, written in the early 50s, already reflects this kind of interplay between worship, doctrine, and ethics and the difficulty in making the connections between them:

> Now in the following instructions I do not commend you, because when you come together it is not for the better but for the worse. For, to begin with, when you come together as a church, I hear that there are divisions among you; and to some extent I believe it. Indeed, there have to be factions among you, for only so will it become clear who among you are genuine. When you come together, it is not really to eat the Lord's supper. For when the time comes to eat, each of you goes ahead with your own supper, and one goes hungry and another becomes drunk. What! Do you not have homes to eat and drink in? Or do you show contempt for the church of God and humiliate those who have nothing? What should I say to you? Should I commend you? In this matter I do not commend you!
>
> For I received from the Lord what I also handed on to you, that the Lord Jesus on the night when he was betrayed took a loaf of bread, and when he had given thanks, he broke it and said, "This is my body that is for you. Do this in remembrance of me." In the same way he took the cup also, after supper, saying, "This cup is the new covenant in my blood. Do this, as often as you drink it, in remembrance of me." For as often as you eat this bread and drink the cup, you proclaim the Lord's death until he comes.
>
> Whoever, therefore, eats the bread or drinks the cup of the Lord in an unworthy manner will be answerable for the body and blood of the Lord. Examine yourselves, and only then eat of the bread and drink of the cup. For all who eat and drink without discerning the body, eat and drink judgment against themselves. For this reason many of you are weak and ill, and some have died. But if we judged ourselves, we would not be judged. But when we are judged by the Lord, we are disciplined so that we may not be condemned along with the world.
>
> So then, my brothers and sisters, when you come together to eat, wait for one another. If you are hungry, eat at home, so that when you come together, it will not be for your condemnation. About the other things I will give instructions when I come.

James Dallen offers an excellent description of the contents and context of this eleventh chapter, writing:

> The Corinthian Christians . . . celebrated the Lord's Supper as the common meal of the Christian family. As Paul saw it, unity was

their basic characteristic as a Christian community and the meal showed that unity. By who they were and how they took responsibility for one another they stood in sharp contrast with the world outside Christ: they were a new creation, a new humanity, the Second Adam—humanity as God intends it to be when the work of creation is completed. But when the Corinthians came together, instead of sharing their contributions and showing their common unity they went separate ways. The well-off came (pardon the anachronisms!) with their smoked pheasant and *Ile de France* bread, their chilled *Chateauneuf-du-Pape* wine and linen in wicker baskets. They spread their cloth and reclined in congenial company, with one another. And the poor brought their baloney sandwiches and diet *Cokes* in brown paper bags and huddled together, with occasional envious glances at their betters.[12]

We know Paul's response to this divisive ritual behavior clearly. Whatever it was that the Corinthian Christians were claiming to do, it was, according to him, most assuredly not the *Lord's* Supper that was occurring in their assemblies. And what they didn't get straight was the connection of the meal to the community sharing the meal, especially the poor among them. In fact, as modern biblical scholars tell us, the *body* Paul calls them to discern is not the Body and Blood of Christ in the eucharistic elements but the *body* the Supper serves to build up, namely, the community that, for Paul, *is* that Body of Christ. Not to discern *this* body, not to discern the divisions within that community, but to perpetuate them even in the liturgical assembly was to eat and drink judgment and condemnation upon themselves.[13] What Paul calls for, then, is both a renewal of the liturgical and doctrinal

---

[12] James Dallen, "Liturgy and Justice for All," *Worship* 65, no. 4 (1991): 291.

[13] On this, see Alan Kreider and Eleanor Kreider, *Worship and Mission after Christendom* (Scotdale, PA: Herald Press, 2011), 91–108. For standard treatments of the relationship between the Christian community and the poor in St. Paul's letters, see Bruce W. Longenecker, *Remember the Poor: Paul, Poverty, and the Greco-Roman World* (Grand Rapids, MI: Eerdmans, 2010); Wayne Meeks, *The Origins of Christian Morality: The First Two Centuries* (New Haven, CT: Yale University Press, 1995); and idem, *The First Urban Christians: The Social World of the Apostle Paul*, 2nd ed. (New Haven, CT: Yale University Press, 2003). See also Daniel G. Groody, *Globalization, Spirituality, and Justice: Navigating the Path to Peace* (Maryknoll, NY: Orbis Books, 2007), 31–58.

meaning of the Eucharist and a renewal of the community that assembles to celebrate that Eucharist.

It is not that Paul is giving the Corinthian Christians some kind of new doctrinal teaching about the Eucharist. Rather, he is reminding them of what he had already handed on to them at some point before about the meaning of their meal fellowship. Several years ago in his book *Real Presence*, Regis Duffy interpreted this as Paul making use of the *lex orandi* argument in his critique of the Corinthian community, which was seeking to hide behind its worship "as the luxury of the saved" rather than embracing "the further acceptance of the saving death of Jesus and its deepened meaning for [their] shared lives,"[14] which the meal was all about. Consequently, in Corinth,

> [Paul] saw a practical situation, which was directly opposed to Gospel teaching: the insensitivity of the rich continued to oppress the poor even in the very rituals that, theoretically, were to make all one because Christ had died for all. Nowhere in his analysis of the Corinthian problem did Paul suggest that God was absent from the Corinthians' celebrations. *Rather, Paul accused these Christians of using the signs of God's presence (liturgy) to avoid his presence.* It was the Corinthians, in fact, who were absent in spirit from the celebration of God's presence.[15]

Although Paul's address to the Corinthians regarding their meal fellowship usually receives the greatest amount of attention in the study of New Testament texts about the Eucharist apart from the gospels, there are other similar examples elsewhere. One of those texts that appears to be addressed again precisely to a liturgical assembly is the Letter of James. And, like Paul, James also displays a deep concern for the relationship between rich and poor in the Christian community and the care of that community for widows and orphans. In the following text James refers precisely to the relationship between worship and ethics:

> Every generous act of giving, with every perfect gift, is from above, coming down from the Father of lights, with whom there is no variation or shadow due to change. In fulfillment of his own purpose he

[14] Regis Duffy, *Real Presence: Worship, Sacraments, and Commitment* (San Francisco: Harper & Row, 1982), 9.
[15] Ibid., 6.

gave us birth by the word of truth, so that we would become a kind of first fruits of his creatures.

You must understand this, my beloved: let everyone be quick to listen, slow to speak, slow to anger; for your anger does not produce God's righteousness. Therefore rid yourselves of all sordidness and rank growth of wickedness, and welcome with meekness the implanted word that has the power to save your souls.

But be doers of the word, and not merely hearers who deceive themselves. For if any are hearers of the word and not doers, they are like those who look at themselves in a mirror; for they look at themselves and, on going away, immediately forget what they were like. But those who look into the perfect law, the law of liberty, and persevere, being not hearers who forget but doers who act—they will be blessed in their doing.

If any think they are religious, and do not bridle their tongues but deceive their hearts, their religion is worthless. Religion that is pure and undefiled before God, the Father, is this: to care for orphans and widows in their distress, and to keep oneself unstained by the world.

My brothers and sisters, do you with your acts of favoritism really believe in our glorious Lord Jesus Christ? For if a person with gold rings and in fine clothes comes into your assembly, and if a poor person in dirty clothes also comes in, and if you take notice of the one wearing the fine clothes and say, "Have a seat here, please," while to the one who is poor you say, "Stand there," or, "Sit at my feet," have you not made distinctions among yourselves, and become judges with evil thoughts? Listen, my beloved brothers and sisters. Has not God chosen the poor in the world to be rich in faith and to be heirs of the kingdom that he has promised to those who love him? But you have dishonored the poor. Is it not the rich who oppress you? Is it not they who drag you into court? Is it not they who blaspheme the excellent name that was invoked over you? (Jas 1:22–2:7)

What is of particular interest here is that James is actually offering what can certainly be called a "liturgical" theology. His statement in 1:27, "Religion that is pure and undefiled before God, the Father, is this: to care for orphans and widows in their distress, and to keep oneself unstained by the world," is actually a statement about worship and/or the Christian cult. The word translated, unfortunately, by most as "religion," which, while accurate, is actually Θρεσκεία (*threskeia*), a word also translatable as "cultus" or "worship." "Religion" for James, then, has the connotations of worship, and the acceptable worship of God has this ethical component issuing in care for orphans and widows, in short, for all those dependent on the care of the Christian community so that the poor chosen by God for salvation are not "dishonored" by the community as they seek to avoid favoritism toward the rich in their liturgical gatherings.

What is often *not* noted about James' approach, especially, it must be said, by Protestant theologians who tend to dismiss him outright as a proponent of "works" over faith, is that his perspective is grounded firmly in baptism and so rooted actually in God, the giver of all good gifts (1:22). For, he says in 1:23, "in fulfillment of his own purpose he gave us birth by the word of truth, so that we would become a kind of first fruits of his creatures." And, clearly, "birth by the word of truth" is James' reference to baptism.[16] Hence, while James might differ with Paul over the definition of faith and, hence, the relationship of works to faith, it does seem that both share a rather common "liturgical" theology.

In his letters, as Robert Taft notes,[17] Paul never uses cultic or worship language for anything other than the work of Christ himself and our life lived in Christ: "I appeal to you therefore, brothers and sisters, by the mercies of God to present your bodies as a living sacrifice, holy and acceptable to God, which is your spiritual worship. Do not be conformed to this world, but be transformed by the renewing of your minds, so that you may discern what is the will of God—what is good and acceptable and perfect" (Rom 12:1-2) And, like James, Paul grounds that transformation and living out of that self-sacrificial life in Christ in baptism. The classic text illustrating this, of course, is Romans 6:3-11:

> Do you not know that all of us who have been baptized into Christ Jesus were baptized into his death? Therefore we have been buried with him by baptism into death, so that, just as Christ was raised from the dead by the glory of the Father, so we too might walk in newness of life.

---

[16] I owe the insights about θρεσκεία and baptism in this section of James to Reginald H. Fuller and Daniel Westberg, *Preaching the Lectionary: The Word of God for the Church of Today*, 3rd ed. (Collegeville, MN: Liturgical Press, 2006), 349.

[17] See Robert Taft, "Toward a Theology of the Christian Feast," in idem, *Beyond East and West: Problems in Liturgical Understanding*, 2nd rev. and enlarged ed. (Rome: Pontifical Oriental Institute, 1997), 21.

For if we have been united with him in a death like his, we will certainly be united with him in a resurrection like his. We know that our old self was crucified with him so that the body of sin might be destroyed, and we might no longer be enslaved to sin. For whoever has died is freed from sin. But if we have died with Christ, we believe that we will also live with him. We know that Christ, being raised from the dead, will never die again; death no longer has dominion over him. The death he died, he died to sin, once for all; but the life he lives, he lives to God. So you also must consider yourselves dead to sin and alive to God in Christ Jesus.

It is not often noted that when St. Paul speaks of baptism in the above text he does not say that we are dead, buried, *and risen* already in Christ. Rather, what he *does* say is that we are dead and buried in Christ by baptism with the result that "*if* we have been united with him in a death like his, we *will* certainly be united with him in a resurrection like his" (Rom 6:5, emphasis added). Resurrection thus remains a future reality, a reality not yet accomplished or fulfilled but one in which we now walk in "newness of life." In other words, for Paul, in this context, baptism is really about our participation in the death and burial of Christ in the *hope* of our ultimate resurrection in him. Or, as he writes in Galatians 2:19-20, "I have been crucified with Christ; and it is no longer I who live, but it is Christ who lives in me. And the life I live in the flesh I live by faith in the Son of God, who loved me and gave himself for me," or, as we read in the deutero-Pauline letter to the Colossians, "for you have died, and your life is hidden with Christ in God" (3:3). If the letter to the Colossians moves already toward including our resurrection as part of the baptismal event, Paul's own theology in Galatians and Romans does not. Clearly, for him, the profound reality of baptism means that whatever our life is now after baptism or whatever it will be at the resurrection, it is this death and burial, this participation in *Christ's* crucifixion, death, and burial, that marks our present, we might say "cruciform," existence in the world as the cross of Christ itself continues to characterize and shape that existence. While this baptismal reality certainly gives rise to those powerful metaphors of conversion to Christ, of constant dying to sin and being raised up to walk in newness of life with and in Christ, of putting to death the "old Adam," and of a life of continual and ongoing conversion, repentance, and renewal, one thing is most clear. For

St. Paul, the baptized are already "dead" and "buried." Whatever the future holds in Christ, because of baptism, death itself is a reality and experience already *behind* us! And that has profound consequences for how the baptized face and embrace the postbaptismal life itself in their cruciform journey toward the resurrection. For, because of baptism, Christians are formed and commissioned to be in the world as Christ was in the world, as one who came to serve others and not be served by others. The ethic of life then flowing from baptism is nothing other than life lived in Christ, a life that is to be lived for others!

The references above to baptism in both James and Paul bring with them another question related to what appears to be the orientation of the Christian meal fellowship toward ministry to the poor, including *especially* widows and orphans in the Greco-Roman context of the first century. That question concerns the identity of the participants in the meal fellowship themselves and whether there were any "requirements" for entry into that fellowship. Who reclined at table with the Christian communities in their meal fellowship? Is it true, to paraphrase a modern popular liturgical song, that "all were welcome" at the table of the Lord? In spite of the developing modern pastoral approach to this topic within a variety of different churches now practicing an "open communion" for everyone, baptized or not, and basing that practice on what the Jesus of history is purported to have done in his own inclusive table fellowship,[18] the fact is, as Lathrop notes correctly, that we really have no idea at all about the meals of the Christian communities before 1 Corinthians 11.[19] And while the meal described there is certainly inclusive of rich and poor, it is the rich and poor who, in the wider context of 1 Corinthians, are clearly part of the baptized, although 1 Corinthians 14:22-25 does envision the possibility of "outsiders" and "unbelievers" coming into the assembly.[20] And if we take the witness of the gospels here as words addressed to Christian meal fellowships by the evangelists, we must also take seriously the fact that, several years after 1 Corinthians, they too are addressed to the *baptized* who constitute those fellowships.

---

[18] The primary advocate of Jesus' inclusive table fellowship was, of course, Norman Perrin, *Rediscovering the Teaching of Jesus* (San Francisco: Harper & Row, 1976).

[19] Lathrop, *The Four Gospels on Sunday*, 55.

[20] See Kreider and Kreider, *Worship and Mission*, 104–5.

Further, all four of those gospels begin the narrative of Christ's life at the Jordan with his baptism by John (Mark 1:9-11; Matt 3:13-17; Luke 3:21-22; and John 1:29-34), a baptism that Christian initiation scholars interpret as reflecting Christian baptisms in the late first century. Is this not done deliberately so that the meal fellowships themselves might see their own baptisms as constituting their foundational identity in Christ? Further, the gospels themselves tend to be concerned about baptism and not only about meals. In Matthew's "Great Commission" (Matt 28), it is baptism that is commanded as the Matthean church moves into the Gentile world. In Mark, baptism is itself the interpretative word about the cross and the meal in 10:35ff. where Jesus asks James and John whether they are able to share his baptism and drink his cup. And baptism is so important in the Gospel of John that Jesus himself is presented three times as a baptizer (John 3:22, 26; 4:1), and, if not Jesus himself, as John 4:2 wants to claim, there can be no question but that the Fourth Gospel certainly associates Jesus and his disciples as part of a baptizing movement akin to that of John the Baptist and his disciples.

In other words, speculation about whether the historical Jesus invited "everybody" to the table is precisely that: *speculation*. Even those several meal settings in the gospels that might be taken as evidence of Jesus' own inclusive, egalitarian table fellowship, as Andrew McGowan has demonstrated, show Jesus generally not as *host* but rather as *guest* at the meals of others.[21] But even with regard to those meal contexts where Jesus does assume the role of host (e.g., his several feeding miracles and the Emmaus account in Luke 24), Michael Tuck has noted recently:

> In all of these stories, *before we have the feeding*, we have responses to Jesus on the part of those who later become the participants in the meal. The response could be curiosity, as it was among the crowds.

[21] Andrew McGowan, "The Meals of Jesus and the Meals of the Church: Eucharistic Origins and Admission to Communion," in *Studia Liturgica Diversa: Essays in Honor of Paul F. Bradshaw*, ed. Maxwell E. Johnson and L. Edward Phillips (Portland, OR: Pastoral Press, 2004), 101–16. See also the helpful essay by Jan Michael Joncas, "Tasting the Kingdom of God: The Meal Ministry of Jesus and Its Implications for Contemporary Worship and Life," *Worship* 74, no. 4 (2000): 329–65.

It could be repentance . . . or it could be divine inspiration and love as it was in the story of the road to Emmaus. It could be any of these reactions and more, but the stories indicate that some sort of reaction or response to the person of Jesus comes before the invitation to the messianic banquet. . . . Meals also appear prominently in Jesus' teaching, most notably in the image of the wedding feast. . . . Again, these stories seem to tell us about a radical invitation offered to those who ordinarily would not be invited. But this invitation is not without some qualifications; we must respond appropriately to the invitation.[22]

Hence, the most we can conclude is that those who reclined at the Christian table as part of the meal fellowship were baptized Christians and those assemblies themselves are being challenged by the New Testament writers to live out the implications of their meal sharing by ministry to the poor, both within and outside of the fellowship. In other words, if the meals of Christians appeared to be inclusive, with Jew and Greek, slave and free, male and female (Gal 4), it is not because the churches were in any social position to have everyone come but because it was *baptism* that was inclusive and open to all. Even before the end of the New Testament period—and contemporaneous with some of the Gospels—this question was already addressed by the Syrian proto-church order, the *Didache*, where we read, "do not let anyone eat or drink of your Eucharist except those baptized into the name of the Lord" (*Didache* 9). Whether this reflects some kind of shift in practice from a more inclusive one is hard to say. But it is surely consistent with what is implied in the New Testament writings as well.

Furthermore, whatever issues there may have been about participants in Christian meal sharing in the first century, beyond the presence of rich and poor in the same assembly, such as at Corinth or reflected in the Letter of James, the only real question here seems to have been whether Jewish Christians and Gentile Christians could share table companionship together, an issue reflected both in the Acts of the Apostles and in Galatians. With regard to *this* sort of inclusivity at meals, Nathan Mitchell is certainly correct when he says:

[22] Michael Tuck, "Who Is Invited to the Feast? A Critique of the Practice of Communion without Baptism," *Worship* 86, no. 6 (2012): 505–27, here at 520–21; emphasis added.

Many of the practices and beliefs we modern Christians take for granted were not so obvious to the earliest generations of believers. Among these was the ticklish question of whether Jewish and Gentile Christians could sit down together at the same table. (For many Jews, eating with Gentiles would have meant breaking God's law and becoming unclean.) Was eucharistic dining destined to be a *barrier* separating persons along racial and ethnic lines, or would it become a *bridge* bringing them together? Underlying this question were even more basic questions: Should the Christian community be a closed one, or one that is multicultural, multi-ethnic and racially diverse? Are the disciples of Jesus radically exclusive or inclusive? . . . Christians such as the evangelist Mark came down strongly on the side of *inclusivity*, and they structured their reports of Jesus' meals to support this point of view. In so doing, Mark redefined discipleship and holiness in terms of food. Becoming a disciple, participating in the new kind of holiness envisioned by Jesus, meant taking part in an inclusive table fellowship. It entailed a revolutionary (and highly controversial) understanding of social status and hierarchy. It meant associating with—and offering the reign (presence) of God to—persons who, by the normal standards of Judaism, were wicked. The primary personal and social virtue sought among the members of this newly emergent, culturally/racially/ethnically diversified community was to be *diakonia*, service at table, the work of a slave.[23]

But here as well, it must be noted, we are dealing with the baptized, with those who are already disciples, and not with "everyone," even if the implication of this inclusive, baptized, meal-sharing community is that the participants are to show the same hospitality and welcome to those seeking entrance into this inclusive table fellowship through conversion and baptism. In short, it is *not* that meal fellowship leads somehow to baptism but, rather, that baptism leads to the table, at least, according to what we can know from the writings of the New Testament.

2. *Lex Orandi, Lex Credendi, Lex Agendi* and the Early Churches

The same kind of concern for the connection between what happens in worship and what the implications of worship are for ethics, or

---

[23] Nathan Mitchell, *Eucharist as Sacrament of Initiation*, Forum Essays 2 (Chicago: Liturgy Training Publications, 1994), 99–100.

how ethics "authenticates" or "verifies" worship, is clearly reflected in various places in the first five centuries of the church's history. And, of course, our earliest nonbiblical reference to this comes from the much-quoted description of the eucharistic liturgy by Justin Martyr (d. 165) in his *First Apology*:

> After these [services] we constantly remind each other of these things. *Those who have more come to the aid of those who lack, and we are constantly together.* Over all that we receive we bless the Maker of all things through his Son Jesus Christ and through the Holy Spirit. And on the day called Sunday there is a meeting in one place of those who live in cities or the country, and the memoirs of the apostles or the writings of the prophets are read as long as time permits. When the reader has finished, the president in a discourse urges and invites [us] to the imitation of these noble things. Then we all stand up together and offer prayers. And, as said before, when we have finished the prayer, bread is brought, and wine and water, and the president similarly sends up prayers and thanksgivings to the best of his ability, and the congregation assents, saying the Amen; the distribution, and reception of the consecrated [elements] by each one, takes place and they are sent to the absent by the deacons. *Those who prosper, and who so wish, contribute, each one as much as he chooses to. What is collected is deposited with the president, and he takes care of orphans and widows, and those who are in want on account of sickness or any other cause, and those who are in bonds, and the strangers who are sojourners among [us], and, briefly, he is the protector of all those in need.* We all hold this common gathering on Sunday.[24]

Like James, Justin's concern appears to be with those in need within the Christian community itself rather than those outside it. Nevertheless, this is an important enough characteristic of the Sunday Eucharist for Justin that he makes a point of it in this description, which, after all, is intended for the reading of the pagan emperor Antoninus Pius. While Justin does not indicate *where* in the structure of the eucharistic liturgy this "collection" is made, if anywhere *in* the liturgy itself, such a collection on behalf of widows, orphans, and others is certainly a constitutive element of the meal fellowship of Justin's local

---

[24] *First Apology* 67, in Edward Rochie Hardy, LCC, 1, 287; emphasis added.

community in Rome.[25] Similar concern for the poor in the liturgical assembly is also evident in the *Didascalia Apostolorum*, with special regard therein for the role of the bishop. In words echoing James 2:2-4, *Didascalia Apostolorum* 12 directs:

> If a poor man or a poor woman comes, whether they are from your own parish or another, especially if they are advanced in years, and there should be no room for them, then make a place for them, O bishop, with all your heart, even if you yourself have to sit on the ground. You must not make any distinction between persons, if you wish your ministry to be pleasing to God.[26]

One of the ways that Christians were formed liturgically in the church's ministry to widows and orphans, and ministry to the poor in general, was through the process known as the prebaptismal catechumenate. Unfortunately, we are not completely certain about the overall *contents* of specific catechetical instruction provided to catechumens within the churches of the first three centuries. From scattered references throughout early Christian writings, however, it is quite clear that in addition to some kind of explanation of the Scriptures in relation to salvation in Christ, ethical or moral formation in the life of the Christian community was an essential component in this process. That is, as it is often said, the catechumenate was an apprenticeship in Christian discipleship. The first six chapters of the *Didache*, for example, describe what is called "The Two Ways," that of life and death. Significantly, the contents of these first six chapters are not concerned with Christian *doctrine* at all but focus on the Ten Commandments, the Sermon on the Mount, and the type of ethical-moral life expected from those who are to be members of Christ through baptism. The "Way of Death," in fact, includes several examples of people:

> who do not show mercy to a poor person, who are not distressed by [the plight of] the oppressed, who do not know him who made them, [who are] child murderers, who destroy what God has formed, who

---

[25] In his *Holy Things: A Liturgical Theology* (Minneapolis: Fortress Press, 1993), 45ff., Gordon Lathrop makes this emphasis on the poor a "third focus" in his suggestion of a liturgical *ordo* constituted by the other two *foci*, namely, word and meal.

[26] Lucien Deiss, *Springtime of the Liturgy: Liturgical Texts of the First Four Centuries* (Collegeville, MN: Liturgical Press, 1979), 176.

turn away from the needy person, who oppress the person who is distressed, [who are] defenders of the rich [and] unjust judges of the poor—[. . . who are] sinners in everything that they do.[27]

Later in history, at least by the middle of the fourth century, though possibly reflecting a much earlier stratum here,[28] chapter 20 of the so-called *Apostolic Tradition* refers to an examination of those who have completed the catechumenate and now desire to enter the next stage of the process—"election"—leading more immediately to baptism. Again, the questions they are asked at this point are questions not about doctrine but about the quality of their lives. Chapter 20 directs:

> And (δέ) when those appointed to receive baptism (βάπτισμα) are chosen, their life (βίος) having been examined (if they lived virtuously [- σεμνός] while they were catechumens [κατηχούμενος], and if they honored the widows [χήρα] and if they visited those who are sick, and if they fulfilled every good work), and when those brought them in testify in his [sic] behalf that he acted thus, then let them hear the gospel (εὐαγγέλιον).[29]

Paul Bradshaw has drawn attention to this concern for the poor in Justin Martyr and the early church orders, especially the *Didache* and so-called *Apostolic Tradition*, writing:

> The so-called *Apostolic Tradition* also gives instructions both about supper being given for the benefit of the poor and about donations of food being made to them to take home (chapters 28, 30), both of which . . . were common cultural practices, while *Didache* 13.4 directs that in the absence of prophets in a Christian community to be the recipients of the firstfruits that have been offered, they are to be donated to the poor. . . . Although the reception of communion

---

[27] *Didache* 5.2, in Kurt Niederwimmer, *The Didache*, trans. Linda M. Maloney, Hermeneia Commentary Series (Minneapolis: Fortress Press, 1998), 115.

[28] See Paul F. Bradshaw, Maxwell E. Johnson, and L. Edward Phillips, *The Apostolic Tradition: A Commentary*, Hermeneia Commentary Series (Minneapolis: Fortress Press, 2002), 109.

[29] Ibid., 104. The text translated does not appear in the earlier Latin version of the document. Here the translation is based on the Sahidic Coptic version from its eleventh-century manuscript.

was restricted to the baptized, . . . this does not mean that charitable feeding was limited only to those persons. It is important to note that while *Apostolic Tradition* 27.1 directs that catechumens are not to "sit at the table of the Lord with believers," chapter 26.2 does include them in some eating and drinking, but with "exorcized bread" and their own cup because they are not yet pure. . . . The presence of a prohibition against the unbaptized sharing the Eucharist in *Didache* 9.5 could also be thought to imply that they were there at that event. . . . The earliest Christian Eucharistic meal, therefore . . . was itself a practical expression of . . . love, as those who had means fed those in the community who were hungry, sending them home with left-overs to sustain them during the week and distributing portions to those unable to be present. It was no wonder then that one of the names used to designate that meal in some Christian communities was *agape*—the Greek word for "love."[30]

This concern remains in all of those church orders derived from the so-called *Apostolic Tradition*, namely, the *Canons of Hippolytus*, the *Apostolic Constitutions*, and the *Testamentum Domini*. Even when more explicit instruction on the creeds became a significant component of the catechumenal process, such as, for example, in the prebaptismal catecheses of Cyril of Jerusalem and Ambrose of Milan, part of the election process for those entering into the final phase of preparation for baptism now as *electi, compententes*, or *photizomenoi*, still included, as the late fourth-century Spanish pilgrim Egeria notes, an examination of the candidate's moral life before election.[31] It may well be that it was the catechumenate itself that functioned in Christian antiquity as forming people in the *lex agendi*.

In addition to the catechumenate, one of the other key places where this sort of concern was frequently addressed is in homilies given at the eucharistic liturgy. Already in the middle of the second century Clement of Alexandria, in his "Who Is the Rich Man That Can Be Saved?"[32] connects eucharistic participation with ethics:

---

[30] Paul F. Bradshaw, *Reconstructing Early Christian Worship* (Collegeville, MN: Liturgical Press, Pueblo, 2010), 23.

[31] See *Peregrinatio Egeriae* 45.1–4, in John Wilkinson, trans., *Egeria's Travels* (London: SPCK, 1971), 161–62.

[32] GCS *Clemens* 3. Translation from ANF, 2, 591–604.

23. Hear the Savior: "I regenerated thee, who wert ill born by the world to death. I emancipated, healed, ransomed thee. I will show thee the face of the good Father God. Call no man thy father on earth. Let the dead bury the dead; but follow thou Me. For I will bring thee to a rest of ineffable and unutterable blessings, which eye hath not seen, nor ear heard, nor have entered into the heart of men; into which angels desire to look, and see what good things God hath prepared for the saints and the children who love Him. I am He who feeds thee, giving Myself as bread, of which he who has tasted experiences death no more, and supplying day by day the drink of immortality. I am teacher of super celestial lessons. For thee I contended with Death, and paid thy death, which thou owedst for thy former sins and thy unbelief towards God."

Indeed, what Christ has done in baptism and continues to do in the Eucharist is the very catalyst for ministry to the poor:

13. And how much more beneficial the opposite case, for a man, through possessing a competency, both not himself to be in straits about money, and also to give assistance to those to whom it is requisite so to do! For if no one had anything, what room would be left among men for giving? And how can this dogma fail to be found plainly opposed to and conflicting with many other excellent teachings of the Lord? "Make to yourselves friends of the mammon of unrighteousness, that when ye fail, they may receive you into the everlasting habitations." "Acquire treasures in heaven, where neither moth nor rust destroys, nor thieves break through." How could one give food to the hungry, and drink to the thirsty, clothe the naked, and shelter the houseless, for not doing which He threatens with fire and the outer darkness, if each man first divested himself of all these things? Nay, He bids Zaccheus and Matthew, the rich tax-gathers, entertain Him hospitably. And He does not bid them part with their property, but, applying the just and removing the unjust judgment, He subjoins, "To-day salvation has come to this house, forasmuch as he also is a son of Abraham." He so praises the use of property as to enjoin, along with this addition, the giving a share of it, to give drink to the thirsty, bread to the hungry, to take the houseless in, and clothe the naked. But if it is not possible to supply those needs without substance, and He bids people abandon their substance, what else would the Lord be doing than exhorting to give and not to give the same things, to feed and not to feed, to take in and to shut out, to share and not to share which were the most irrational of all things.

14. Riches, then, which benefit also our neighbors, are not to be thrown away. For they are possessions, inasmuch as they are possessed, and goods, inasmuch as they are useful and provided by God for the use of men; and they lie to our hand, and are put under our power, as material and instruments which are for good use to those who know the instrument. If you use it skillfully, it is skillful; if you are deficient in skill, it is affected by your want of skill, being itself destitute of blame. Such an instrument is wealth. Are you able to make a right use of it? It is subservient to righteousness. Does one make a wrong use of it? It is, on the other hand, a minister of wrong. For its nature is to be subservient, not to rule. That then which of itself has neither good nor evil, being blameless, ought not to be blamed; but that which has the power of using it well and ill, by reason of its possessing voluntary choice. And this is the mind and judgment of man, which has freedom in itself and self-determination in the treatment of what is assigned to it. So let no man destroy wealth, rather than the passions of the soul, which are incompatible with the better use of wealth. So that, becoming virtuous and good, he may be able to make a good use of these riches. The renunciation, then, and selling of all possessions, is to be understood as spoken of the passions of the soul.

In addition to Clement of Alexandria, two later patristic homilists stand out, namely, John Chrysostom in Antioch and Augustine in Hippo, North Africa.[33] John Chrysostom's famous *Sermon 50* from his *Sermons on Matthew* offers a particularly strong identification of the relationship between Christ and the poor incumbent upon those who celebrate the Eucharist:

> Do you want to honor Christ's Body? Then do not scorn him naked now, honoring him here in church with silk vestments but neglecting him out there where he is cold and naked. He who said, "This is my

---

[33] On the attitude toward the poor in the period after Constantine and how the rich were now encouraged by the bishops not to renounce their wealth but to use it in almsgiving, in building churches, and in various bequests to churches and shrines, especially those of the martyrs, see Peter Brown's now definitive study, *Through the Eye of a Needle: The Fall of Rome, and the Making of Christianity in the West, 350–550 AD* (Princeton, NJ: Princeton University Press, 2012). See also idem, *Power and Persuasion in Late Antiquity: Towards a Christian Empire* (Madison: University of Wisconsin Press, 1992), 71–117. See also Groody, *Globalization, Spirituality, and Justice*, 59–90.

Body," also said, "You saw me hungry and did not feed me." The deed we do here in church requires a pure heart, not splendid vestments; but the deed we do out there requires great concern and effort.

Let us become wise, then, and honor Christ as he wishes. The sweetest honor for anyone is the honor he really wants, not the honor others may mistakenly choose to give him. Peter thought to honor Christ by refusing to let him wash his feet; yet to Christ the refusal was anything but an honor. Show him, then, the honor his commandment requires by giving your riches to the poor. God does not want gold vessels but gold hearts.

I am not trying to prevent you from using gorgeous vestments but only asking you also, and first, to give alms. The Lord accepts the ornaments, but he is much more eager for the alms. Only the offerer profits by the adornments; both the giver and the receiver profit by the alms.

What use is it for Christ to have golden cups on the table if he is dying of hunger? First fill the hungry person; then adorn the table with what is left over. Will you provide a cup of gold and not give a cup of water? What good is it to Christ to have a gold tablecloth when he has no clothes by which to be covered? If you see a man hungry and you abandon him in order to deck the altar with gold for his sake, do you expect him to be grateful to you? If you see people freezing in rags and refuse them clothes but erect golden columns in their names, what response do you expect? Will they not think you are making fools of them?

Think, then, how Christ feels as he wanders homeless. You do not give him a roof, but you build a glorious temple for him! Once again, I am not attacking all these adornments; I am only bidding you to put first things first. No one who has failed to adorn churches has ever been accused by the Lord, but hell awaits those who scorn a brother or sister in need. A brother or sister is a far more precious temple than a church.[34]

Elsewhere in the same *Sermons on Matthew*, Chrysostom actually makes the hands of the poor the dispensers of the olive oil that enables Christians to enter the wedding feast of the Eucharist with their oil lamps properly prepared:

[34] *Benedictine Daily Prayer*, ed. Maxwell E. Johnson and Monks of Saint John's Abbey (Collegeville, MN: Liturgical Press, 2005), 743–44.

Let us also go out to the hands of the poor, for that is the Mount of Olives. The multitude of the poor are the olive-trees planted in the house of God, dripping the oil which needful for us there. The five virgins (Mt 25.1-13) had it, and the rest, who did not, perished for that reason. With it, let us go in, that with bright lamps we may meet the Bridegroom. With it let us go forth from here. Let no inhuman person be present, no one who is cruel and merciless, no one at all who is unclean.[35]

And Augustine of Hippo warns strongly of blasphemy in failing to live in the world in a manner consistent with how one blesses God in church:

To bless God in the churches, brethren, means so to live that each one's life may give glory to God. To bless God in word and curse Him in deed is by no means to bless Him in the churches. Almost all bless Him with their tongues, but not all by their works. But those whose conduct is inconsistent with their profession cause God to be blasphemed.[36]

Commenting directly on Augustine, but with words easily applicable both to Chrysostom and to Clement as well, L. Edward Phillips notes:

Augustine recognized that it is entirely possible for a worshipper formally to bless God with words in church while living a life that does not bear witness to the gospel. For Augustine, this turned the blessing uttered in church into blasphemy. Augustine does not suggest that the blessing in church forms the ethical life; rather, the ethical life authenticates the blessing in church. . . . [T]he most important relationship between liturgy and ethics is not direct or causal, but is to be found on a higher level in their common goal, the faithful service of God.[37]

---

[35] *Homily* 82, in Daniel Sheerin, *The Eucharist*, Message of the Fathers of the Church, 7 (Wilmington, DE: Michael Glazier, 1986), 291.

[36] *St. Augustine on the Psalms*, trans. S. Hebgin and F. Corrigan, Ancient Christian Writers 29 (Westminster: Newman Press, 1960), 252, as cited by L. Edward Phillips, "Liturgy and Ethics," in *Liturgy and Dialogue*, ed. Paul Bradshaw and Bryan Spinks (London: SPCK, 1993), 86.

[37] Ibid., 98.

If the connection between worship and ethics was made frequently in early Christian catechumenal formation and homilies, however, another area not to be overlooked is the developing sense of the eucharistic liturgy itself as somehow embodying the church's offering, oblation, or sacrifice. Our earliest explicit reference to viewing the Eucharist in some way as sacrificial is *Didache* 14.1–3, where reconciliation among members of the community is joined to offering the pure sacrifice:

> Assembling on every Sunday of the Lord, break bread and give thanks, confessing your faults beforehand, so that your sacrifice (θυσία) may be pure. Let no one engaged in a dispute with his comrade join you until they have been reconciled lest your sacrifice be profaned. This is [the meaning] of what was said by the Lord: "to offer me a pure sacrifice in every place and time, because I am a great king," says the Lord, "and my name is held in wonder among the nations."[38]

While the *Didache* does not offer an interpretation of the word "sacrifice," scholars conclude that this reference, along with others, has as its primary meaning the "offering" of prayer and praise. Such offering of prayer and praise becomes interpreted in early Christianity as the "bloodless" or "unbloody" sacrifice of Christians in distinction to their Greco-Roman context, where blood sacrifices were the norm. The second-century apologist Athenagoras makes this contrast between Christian pagan sacrifices explicit when he calls the Christian offering both the "bloodless sacrifice" and the "spiritual worship" (Rom 12:1) within the context of the "lifting up of holy hands" in prayer and praise. The same words are used by the second-century *Testament of Levi* 6.3 to refer to the heavenly sacrifice offered by the angels to God,[39] and the mid-third-century *Strasbourg Papyrus* from Egypt, quite possibly a complete eucharistic prayer consisting of praise, offering, and intercession (but no narrative of institution), makes use of the same terminology, including the reference to Malachi 1:11, cited also in *Didache* 14.

[38] Niederwimmer, *The Didache*, 194.

[39] See Robert Daly, *Christian Sacrifice: The Judaeo-Christian Background before Origen*, Studies in Christian Antiquity, vol. 18 (Washington, DC: Catholic University of America Press, 1978), 338–39; and Kenneth Stevenson, *Eucharist and Offering* (New York: Pueblo, 1986), 26–27.

> Giving thanks through him to you with him and the Holy Spirit, we
> offer the reasonable sacrifice and this bloodless service, which all the
> nations offer you, "from sunrise to sunset," from south to north, [for]
> your "name is great among all the nations, and in every place incense
> is offered to your holy name and a pure sacrifice."[40]

Such language regarding the unbloody or bloodless sacrifice as primarily prayer or praise, upon which intercessions for the needs of the
world are based, will be found in later eucharistic prayers, especially
in Egypt. The *Strasbourg Papyrus* provides a clear example of this
since, immediately after the paragraph quoted above, the prayer continues with several intercessions "through this sacrifice and offering."
In his discussion of the development of the Alexandrian eucharistic
prayer known as *Saint Mark*, Geoffrey Cuming added to these early
references above the *Contra Celsum* of Origen ("continually offering
up bloodless sacrifices in his prayers to God"; 8.21) and the *Martyrium
Apollonii* ("I send up the bloodless and pure sacrifice . . . which is
through prayers"; 14.1–3) as further indications of the identification
of prayer and praise with the "unbloody offering."[41] Even when,
along with the citation of Malachi 1:11, the sacrifice becomes associated with the eucharistic gifts and with the sacrifice of Christ in early
patristic literature, as we shall see, the understanding of sacrifice as
verbal prayer and praise does not entirely disappear.[42] For that matter, even the Roman *canon missae* retains this early sense of sacrifice
since its primary focus is the *sacrificium laudis*, the "sacrifice of praise."
As Robert Taft has purportedly said of the contrast between these
unbloody sacrifices of the early Christians and those of the pagans,
"The early Christians weren't in temples killing chickens!" Hence,
there is a strong sense in the first three centuries of what scholars
like Robert Daly and Kenneth Stevenson[43] refer to as the "anti-cultic
bias" regarding the pagan sacrificial cult or what others, like David

[40] Translation from PEER, 53–54.

[41] Cuming, "The Shape of the Anaphora," *Studia Patristica* 20 (1989): 124; and
idem, *The Liturgy of St. Mark*, Orientalia Christiana Analecta 234 (Rome: Pontificio
Istituto Orientale, 1990), 107–8.

[42] For texts see Cuming, *The Liturgy of St. Mark* , 107–8.

[43] See above, note 39.

Power, have called the "words that crack" with regard to sacrificial terminology in Christian eucharistic practice.[44]

Coupled with sacrifice as prayer and praise is the continuation of the New Testament understanding that the very life of Christians is itself the sacrifice Christians are to offer to God in Christ (see Rom 12:1-3). This self-offering in Christ comes to particular expression in the early Christian martyrs who demonstrate by their literal imitation of Christ in his passion the continuation of his own sacrificial offering in the life of the church.[45] Not surprisingly will this come to be associated in a particular way with the Eucharist, an association already made by Ignatius of Antioch in the late first century when he describes his own impending martyrdom in eucharistic terms (temple, libation, altar, etc.).[46] This self-offering comes to further expression in viewing the bread and wine of the Eucharist as elements of creation somehow embodying that offering in the writing of Irenaeus of Lyons, who argues on the basis of the Eucharist for the goodness of creation against the Gnostic devaluation of matter. In his *Adversus Haereses* 4.17.5, he writes:

> The Lord gave directions to his disciples to offer first-fruits to God from God's own creatures, not as though God stood in need of them, but that they themselves may be neither unfruitful nor ungrateful. Thus, he took the bread, which comes from creation, and he gave thanks, saying: "This is my Body." He did likewise with the cup, which is part of the creation to which we ourselves belong, declaring it to be his blood, and [so] he taught the new offering of the new covenant. This is the offering which the church received from the

[44] See David Power, "Words That Crack: The Uses of 'Sacrifice' in Eucharistic Discourse," in *Living Bread, Saving Cup*, ed. R. Kevin Seasoltz (Collegeville, MN: Liturgical Press, 1987), 157–74.

[45] See Candida Moss, *The Other Christs: Imitating Jesus in Ancient Christian Ideologies of Martyrdom* (New York/London: Oxford University Press, 2010); and idem, *Ancient Christian Martyrdom: Diverse Practices, Theologies, and Traditions* (New Haven, CT: Yale University Press, 2012).

[46] See Frederick Klawiter, "The Eucharist and Sacramental Realism in the Thought of St. Ignatius of Antioch," *Studia Liturgica* 37 (2007): 129–63. On martyrdom as constituting a "public liturgy" of sacrifice, a type of public substitution for the domestic eucharistic liturgy, see Robin Darling Young, *In Procession before the World: Martyrdom as Public Liturgy in Early Christianity*, The Pére Marquette Lecture in Theology, 2001 (Milwaukee, WI: Marquette University Press, 2001), 11–12.

apostles and which it offers throughout the whole world, to God who provides us with nourishment, the first-fruits of divine gifts in this new covenant. Of this offering, among the prophets, Malachi had spoken beforehand in these terms: "I have no pleasure in you, says the Lord almighty, and I will not accept sacrifice from your hands. For from the rising of the sun even to its setting my name is glorified among the nations, and in every place incense is offered to my name, and a pure sacrifice; for my name is great among the nations, says the Lord almighty" [Mal 1:10-11]. By these words, he shows in the plainest manner that the former people [the Jews] shall cease to make offering to God, but that in every place sacrifice shall be offered to God, one that is pure, and that God's name is glorified among the nations.[47]

For Irenaeus this eucharistic offering cannot be separated from the lives of those who offer it. In *Adversus* Haereses 18.1 he notes that the "oblation of the church," the "pure sacrifice" of the Eucharist, "is acceptable, not because God needs sacrifice from us, but because those who offer sacrifice are themselves glorified in what they offer, *if the gift be accepted*."[48] And it is clear here that reconciliation with others as commanded in Matthew 5:23-24 is called for in offering an acceptable gift. In *Adversus Haereses* 18.3 he continues, with specific reference to the acceptable sacrifice offered by Abel in Genesis 4, saying:

> For if some endeavor to offer a sacrifice which is clean, correct, and legal according to outward appearances, while not sharing that fellowship with their neighbors which is due, and having no fear of God in their hearts, God is not deceived by that sacrifice which is outwardly correct but hides sin within. Such offering does them no good, but what is wanted is the giving up of the evil conceived within, lest the sin by means of a hypocritical action makes of the giver one's own murderer.[49]

If for Irenaeus, according to Robert Daly,[50] the primary meaning of eucharistic sacrifice was still to be found in the prayer and praise

[47] David Power, trans., *Irenaeus of Lyons on Baptism and Eucharist*, Alcuin/GROW Liturgical Study 18 (Bramcote: Nottingham, 1991),15–16.
[48] Translation from ibid., 17; emphasis added.
[49] Translation from ibid., 18. On this, see further Alan Kreider, "Peacemaking in Worship in the Syrian Church Orders," *Studia Liturgica* 34, no. 2 (2004).
[50] Daly, *Christian Sacrifice*, 339ff.

offered, the reference to Christ's own self-sacrifice by means of the New Testament narrative of institution of the Eucharist made in this context, and the shift toward embodying the oblation in the bread and cup, point ahead clearly to further development in the sacrificial understanding of the Eucharist. Such development is most closely associated with Cyprian of Carthage in mid-third-century North Africa, who takes the influential step of associating the sacrifice of Christ on the cross explicitly with the eucharistic oblation of the church, saying that the Eucharist is done in remembrance of Christ, *"in commemorationem eius"* (*Ep.* 63.2 and 14) and that "the Lord's Passion is the sacrifice that we offer" (*Ep* 63.17). Further:

> if Jesus Christ, our Lord and God, is himself the high priest of God the Father and first offered himself as a sacrifice to the Father, and commanded this to be done in his remembrance, then that priest truly functions in the place of Christ who imitates what Christ did and then offers a true and full sacrifice in the church to God the Father, if he thus proceeds to offer according to what he sees Christ himself to have offered.[51]

Even so, however, if Cyprian's language paved the way for later theologians in this regard, including the more explicit use of offering verbs in association with the bread and cup and the sacrifice of Christ in later eucharistic praying, it is the synthesis of Augustine that appears to capture all of the nuances about the Christian life, unity, charity toward others, and the liturgical expression of the eucharistic sacrifice when he writes in his *City of God* (ca. 420 CE) and in his *Sermon* 272 to the newly baptized (417 CE):

> *City of God* 10: The whole redeemed City itself, that is the congregation and society of the saints, is offered as a universal sacrifice to God by the High Priest, who offered even Himself in suffering for us in the form of a servant, that we might be the body of so great a Head. For this form of a servant did He offer, in this was He offered: for in this is He mediator and priest and sacrifice. And so when the Apostle exhorted us that we should present our bodies a living sacrifice, holy, pleasing to God, our reasonable service [Rom. 12:1] and that we be not

---

[51] *Ep.* 63.14, in Bradshaw and Johnson, *The Eucharistic Liturgies*, 57.

conformed to this world but reformed in the newness of our mind, to prove what is the will of God, that which is good and well-pleasing and complete, which whole sacrifice we ourselves are. . . .

This is the sacrifice of Christians: "the many are one body in Christ." Which also the Church celebrates in the Sacrament of the altar, familiar to the faithful, where it is shown to her that in this thing which she offers she herself is offered. . . .

Thus is He priest, Himself offering, Himself also that which is offered. Of this thing He willed the sacrifice of the Church to be the daily Sacrament; and the Church, since she is the body of the Head Himself, learns to offer herself through Him.[52]

Sermon 272: If you wish to understand the body of Christ, hear the Apostle speaking to the faithful, "Now ye are the body and members of Christ" [I Cor. 12:27]. If you then are the body and members of Christ, your mystery is laid on the Table of the Lord, your mystery you receive. To that which you are you answer Amen, and in answering you assent. For you hear the words, The body of Christ; and you answer Amen. Be a member of the body of Christ, that the Amen may be true. Wherefore then in the bread? Let us assert nothing of our own here; let us listen to the reiterated teaching of the Apostle, who when he spoke of this Sacrament said, "We who are many are one bread, one body" [I Cor. 10:17]; understand and rejoice; unity, truth, goodness, love. "One bread." What is that one bread? "Many are one body." Remember that the bread is not made from one grain but from many. When ye were exorcised, ye were so to speak ground. When ye were baptized, ye were so to speak sprinkled. When ye received the fire of the Holy Ghost, ye were so to speak cooked. Be what you see, and receive what you are. . . . Many grapes hang on the cluster, but the juice of the grapes is gathered together in unity. So also the Lord Christ signified us, wished us to belong to Him, consecrated on His Table the mystery of our peace and unity.[53]

For Augustine the eucharistic offering is the offering of the whole church, Head and members, the *totus Christus*, and that offering implies that what is done or grounded in worship is to be what is done in life, that is, the continual offering of the "reasonable" and "living

[52] *City of God*, book 10 (c. 420), Darwell Stone, *A History of the Doctrine of the Holy Eucharist*, vol. 1 (London: Longmans, Green, 1909), 123–24.

[53] Augustine, *Sermon 272* (c. 415), in Stone, *A History*, vol. 1, 95–96.

sacrifice" (Rom 12:1) of the church expressing that offering in works of charity, works of love. As Joseph Wawrykow has written:

> Augustine's presentation of Eucharist is framed by his understanding of Church as the body of Christ. Christ is the Head of this body; those who are joined to him by faith and charity, having received from Him the Holy Spirit, are His members. In discussing Eucharist, Augustine, first of all, plays up its sign-quality. A sign is a thing that points to another thing (*res*). It signifies that thing, but is not that thing. In the case of the Eucharist, the material elements, the bread and wine point to the *res* that is the power of the sacrament. Taking his cue from 1 Corinthians 10:17, a favorite verse that appears repeatedly throughout his writings, Augustine states that the *res* that is signified by the bread is the Church, the body of Christ, in its fundamental unity, which is grounded in charity. The Eucharist is the sacrament of unity and charity. Just as bread is made out of many grains, so the Church, the body of Christ, is made out of many people who are joined to their Head by their charity.[54]

Worship leads to ethics or moral action, then, because worship is to be expressed in love. Eucharistic sacrifice properly understood, therefore, is not really about a separate "cultic sacrifice" but about life lived in unity with Christ, firmly rooted in the Person and Work of Christ and expressing itself in love. As Alexander Schmemann reminded us years ago:

> Christianity was preached as a saving faith and not as a saving cult. In it the cult was not an object of faith but its result. . . . The cult is only the realization, the actualization of what the believer has already attained by faith, and its whole significance is in the fact that it leads in the Church, the new people of God, created and brought into being by faith.[55]

With regard to what many would consider the problematic notion of eucharistic sacrifice, in the first place, one might surely ask the

---

[54] Joseph Wawrykow, "The Heritage of the Late Empire: Influential Theology," in *A Companion to the Eucharist in the Middle Ages*, ed. Ian Levy, Gary Macy, and Kristen Van Ausdall (Leiden: Brill, 2012), 74–75.

[55] Alexander Schmemann, *Introduction to Liturgical Theology*, 2nd ed. (Crestwood, NY: St. Vladimir's Seminary Press, 1975), 83.

following: Does a sacrificial understanding of the Eucharist issue in a particular ethic or holiness of life? While a *do-ut-des* approach to religious ritual is always a danger, a community that is formed by such a sacrificial understanding may well perceive that its life of ministry and service in and to the world is to be one of sacrificial self-offering in union with Christ, into whose own pattern of self-offering, celebrated and actualized in the Eucharist, they have been and are to be conformed. And in this sense, then, the *lex orandi* of the eucharistic sacrifice, which simply cannot be denied for the first millennium of Christianity, may well be shaping again not only the *lex credendi* but also the *lex agendi*, the self-offering of Christians in the world in service to others.

3. Conclusion

At the beginning of this chapter Nathan Mitchell was quoted as saying that "Christian liturgy begins as ritual practice but ends as ethical performance . . . [the] liturgy of the neighbor verifies liturgy of the church," and that there is need for a *lex agendi* to verify and authenticate both the *lex orandi* and the *lex credendi*. From the Hebrew prophets through Augustine of Hippo we have repeatedly seen this kind of concern for the verification of worship in the very lives of the communities who offer it. Whether the prophetic critique of Amos, the words of ritual critique and reform addressed to early Christian meal fellowships by the gospel and other New Testament writers, catechumenal formation, liturgical homilies, or development in the concept of the Eucharist as the sacrifice of Christ and the church, the concern that Christians live according to how they worship and believe is, indeed, a consistent concern through the ages. And a major part of that concern is directed toward the poor, the widows, the orphans, and the hungry, toward what contemporary Roman Catholic social teaching refers to as the "preferential option for the poor."[56] Such an "ethic" we might even call a "liturgical" or "eucharistic ethic."

When communities and individuals do not verify or authenticate their worship and beliefs in ethical lives consistent with that worship

---

[56] See Bernard Evans, *Lazarus at the Table: Catholics and Social Justice* (Collegeville, MN: Liturgical Press, 2006).

and belief, it is easy to conclude that something must be wrong either with the *lex orandi* or the *lex credendi*. But another conclusion suggests itself as more accurate. In dealing with the relationship between liturgy and ethics several years ago, Geoffrey Wainwright noted that "in so far as the sacraments, or any form of worship, fail to produce appropriate fruit in the lives of the participants, the failure is due to a lack or refusal on the human side of the encounter with God."[57] That approach seems quite consistent with what we have seen in early Christianity. Although the liturgy often does need reform and renewal and doctrine often requires greater clarity and comprehension, it is most often the case that the "problem" is not with either liturgy or doctrine but with those who celebrate and profess to believe. And the answer to that issue is not the abandonment of the liturgy or the liturgical discipline but nothing other than what the evangelists and other New Testament writers did. That is, if there are divisions between rich and poor, if the ethical life of Christians is not consistent with the church's liturgical claims and confessions, then someone like Paul needs to say, "It is certainly not the *Lord's* Supper we are sharing!" And the continual reform of the community's life can begin again from that acknowledgment and realization.

[57] Wainwright, *Doxology*, 403.

Chapter 5

Conclusion

Praying and Believing Together

With the exception of the previous chapter, this study has been concerned with the role that liturgy or praying plays in the shaping of believing or doctrine in early Christianity. And that is why a certain priority has been given to the liturgy in each of the chapters dealing with grace, the Trinity, Christology, and Mary. The *lex orandi* has been given its pride of place in shaping the *lex credendi*, even if, in the case of the previous chapter, it was not so certain as to which was more influential in forming the Christian moral life. At the same time, the principle of *lex orandi* has not been appealed to as a kind of ideological norm or fundamentalist proposition to which any and all theological or doctrinal discourse must adhere because the *lex orandi* is somehow primary to everything else. No. Rather, as we have seen from the beginning of this study, there has always been a creative interplay between praying and believing, between worship and doctrine, and whatever may be concluded about the *lex orandi* shaping the *lex credendi*, the inverse is equally true even if the liturgical encounter with God in Word and Sacrament is for many, if not most, people the foundational and continuing locus for their faith and life.

That interplay is at work even in the New Testament writings, as we saw in the last chapter when looking at various eucharistic texts in 1 Corinthians 11 and the gospels. That is, even getting back to some kind of original or primary *Ur lex orandi* is impossible or, as I have said on occasion, the only true experience of an original *lex orandi* may have been at the Last Supper, and we cannot be certain historically what happened at that Supper at all. The narratives we have—including the institution of the Eucharist at that event—are all the products either of Paul or of the Synoptic Gospel writers who are writing from a critical theological or doctrinal expression to say something to those communities who are celebrating the meal together already. Hence, what we have even in those texts is the product of both the *lex orandi* and the *lex credendi* functioning together in the life of the earliest Christian communities. There is, in other words, really no such thing as a pure *lex orandi* separate from other factors and theological sources.

As an illustration of this in chapter 1, where it was noted that even the original use of the phrase *"ut legem credendi lex statuat supplicandi"* by Prosper of Aquitaine constituted but *one* argument among several, reference was made to the following statement of Edward Kilmartin, who argued that the separation of the *lex orandi* and the *lex credendi* threatens to obscure the unique value of two different kinds of expression of faith:

> The slogan "law of prayer–law of belief" leaves in suspense which magnitude might be the subject, and which the predicate, in particular instances. Consequently, it seems legitimate to state the axiom in this way: *the law of prayer is the law of belief, and vice versa.* . . . On the one hand, the law of prayer implies a comprehensive, and, in some measure a pre-reflective, perception of the life of faith. On the other hand, the law of belief must be introduced because the question of the value of a particular liturgical tradition requires the employment of theoretical discourse. One must reckon with the limits of the liturgy as lived practice of the faith. History has taught us that forms of liturgical prayer and ritual activity, however orthodox, often had to be dropped or changed to avoid heretical misunderstanding. Moreover, in new historical and cultural situations, the question of the correspondence between the community's understanding of Christian truth, and its expression in the liturgy and that of the authentic whole tradition, must continually be placed. To respond responsibly to this problem, other sources of theology must be introduced along with the liturgical-practical grounding of the knowledge of faith.[1]

And more recently Nathan Mitchell has asserted in a very similar manner:

> [T]he ancient, binary formula *lex orandi, lex credendi* ("the rule of prayer is the rule of faith")—though often invoked to assert the priority of

---

[1] Edward Kilmartin, *Christian Liturgy: Theology and Practice*, vol. 1: *Systematic Theology* (Kansas City: Sheed & Ward, 1988), 97.

doxology over doctrine—is in fact something of a red herring. The formula is flawed from the get-go, because its reasoning is circular: "We *believe*," it asserts, "that the church's public prayer shapes what (and how?) we believe." But such a statement *already expresses* fundamental *convictions—beliefs*—about the nature of both Christ and church, beliefs that make liturgy possible (and obligatory) in the first place. There is a sense, of course, in which it is quite true to say that liturgy is where theology is born—where the church is "caught in the act of being most overtly itself as it stands faithfully in the presence of the One who is both object and source" of its faith—and hence that liturgy alone deserves the moniker *theologia prima.* Still, the *lex orandi, lex credendi* formula suffers from the same limitations that beset all such closed-circuit, binary oppositions. If doxology checks doctrine, might not the reverse be true as well, viz., that doctrine checks doxology?[2]

In the development of trinitarian and christological doctrine in early Christianity, in addition to praying shaping believing, it is precisely "doctrine checking doxology," or "forms of liturgical prayer and ritual activity, however orthodox, [being] dropped or changed to avoid heretical misunderstanding," that we also encounter time and time again. While, for example, as we saw in chapter 2, the uncoordinated form of the doxology at the conclusion of prayers or at the end of psalmody was perfectly orthodox, especially as interpreted by Basil of Caesarea, this uncoordinated form increasingly dropped out of liturgical prayer after the Council of Constantinople and either became in reference to Christ, "through Whom and with Whom all honor and glory . . . ," or was replaced by the coordinated form in both East and West, "Glory to the Father and to the Son and to the Holy Spirit," known in the West by the shorthand, the *"Gloria Patri,"* which is sung repeatedly especially in most of the liturgies of the Christian East, eucharistic and otherwise, although in the Roman Rite traditionally only at the end of psalmody in the Office and in the introit at the Eucharist.

Similarly, whatever the liturgical and/or devotional origins of the title *Theotokos* for the Virgin Mary, in the aftermath of the Council of Ephesus, the term finds its way into the eucharistic prayers almost everywhere in the Christian East and West. Also, in the Eastern rites

[2] Nathan Mitchell, *Meeting Mystery: Liturgy, Worship, and Sacraments* (Maryknoll, NY: Orbis Books, 2006), 223.

the term is frequently used in various litanies in the Eucharist and in the Divine Office, especially in the hymns to Mary in Byzantine Vespers and Orthros (Matins) known as the *Theotokia;*[3] in the conclusion to the various litanies in the Byzantine and Armenian Rites, "Commemorating our all-holy, spotless most highly blessed and glorious Lady the Mother of God [*Theotokos*] and ever-virgin Mary with all the saints, let us commend ourselves and one another and our whole life to Christ our God";[4] and in what is known as the Ninth Ode (sometimes called the *Megalynarion*) in Byzantine Orthros, "O higher than the Cherubim, and more glorious beyond compare than the Seraphim, you gave birth to God the Word in virginity. You are truly the Mother of God: you do we exalt."[5] Christologically as well, we have seen already how the doctrinal positions adopted by the councils of Ephesus and Chalcedon influenced worship both with the introduction of the "Theopaschite" clause to the *Trisagion* among the non-Chalcedonian churches and the hymn *O Monogenes* introduced at Constantinople.

Orthodox trinitarian and christological doctrine continued to shape the liturgical prayer of the church in subsequent years and, in turn, that prayer continued to shape the faith of the church. While, as we have seen, the eucharistic prayers themselves played no discernable role in shaping doctrine at either Nicea or Constantinople,[6] there can be no question that, especially in the East, the eucharistic prayers came to embody in a particular way the Orthodox faith of the church. The use of creeds in worship—whether the Nicene-Constantinopolitan or what came to be known as the Roman or Apostles' Creed—was pretty much limited to prebaptismal catechesis and baptism. Only in the sixth century at Constantinople and in the eleventh at Rome did the Nicene-Constantinopolitan Creed become included within the eucharistic liturgy.[7] Nevertheless, what is known as the Syro-Byzantine pattern

---

[3] See J. Raya and J. de Vinck, *Byzantine Daily Worship: With Byzantine Breviary, the Three Liturgies, Propers of the Day, and Various Offices* (Allendale, NJ: Alleluia Press, 1969), 410–26.

[4] Greek text in LEW, 363.

[5] Translation adapted from Raya and de Vinck, *Byzantine Daily Worship*, 166.

[6] See above, chapter 2, 46ff.

[7] See Paul F. Bradshaw and Maxwell E. Johnson, *The Eucharistic Liturgies: Their Evolution and Interpretation* (Collegeville, MN: Liturgical Press, Pueblo, 2012), 152, 204.

of the eucharistic prayer, clearly parallel to the tripartite structure of the Nicene-Constantinopolitan Creed itself, if not actually modeled to some extent on it, became, thanks to the influence of Constantinople, the primary structure for eucharistic praying in the East, used together with or even replacing extant prayers in other Eastern rites. The anaphora called Byzantine Basil (ByzBAS), and probably put into its final form by Basil himself, as we noted in chapter 2, and so antedating the Council of Constantinople, is an excellent example of this rather full trinitarian creedal shape:

Priest: The grace of our Lord Jesus Christ and the love of the God and Father, and the communion of the Holy Spirit be with you all.

People: And with your spirit.

Priest: Let us lift up our hearts.

People: We have them with the Lord.

Priest: Let us give thanks to the Lord.

People: It is fitting and right <to worship the Father, the Son, and the Holy Spirit, the consubstantial and undivided Trinity>.

And the priest begins the holy anaphora: I AM, Master, Lord God, Father almighty, reverend it is truly fitting and right and befitting the magnificence of your holiness to praise you, to hymn you, to bless you, to worship you, to give you thanks, to glorify you, the only truly existing God, and to offer to you with a contrite heart and a humble spirit this our reasonable service. For it is you who granted us the knowledge of your truth; and who is sufficient to declare your powers, to make all your praises to be heard, or to declare all your wonders at all times? [Master], Master of all, Lord of heaven and earth and all Creation, visible and invisible, you sit on the throne of glory and behold the depths, without beginning, invisible, incomprehensible, infinite, unchangeable, the Father of our Lord Jesus Christ the Great God and savior of our hope, who is the image of your goodness, the identical seal, manifesting you the Father in himself, living Word, true God, before all ages wisdom, life, sanctification, power, the true Light by whom the Holy Spirit was revealed, the spirit of truth, the grace of sonship, the pledge of the inheritance to come, the first fruits of eternal good things, lifegiving power, the fountain of sanctification, by whose enabling the whole rational and spiritual Creation does your service and renders you the unending doxology; for all things are your servants. For angels, archangels, thrones, dominions, principalities, powers, virtues, and the cherubim with many eyes praise you, the seraphim stand around you, each having six wings, and with two covering their own faces, and with two their feet, and with two flying, and crying one to the other with unwearying mouths and never-silent doxologies, *(aloud)* singing the triumphal hymn, crying aloud and saying:

People: Holy, <holy, holy, Lord of Sabaoth; heaven and earth are full of your glory. Hosanna in the highest. Blessed is he who comes in the name of the Lord. Hosanna in the highest.>

The priest says privately: With these blessed powers, Master, lover of men, we sinners also cry and say: you are truly holy and all-holy, and there is no measure of the magnificence of your holiness, and you are holy in all your works, for in righteousness and true judgment you brought all things upon us. For you took dust from the earth and formed man; you honored him with your image, O God, and set him in the paradise of pleasure, and promised him immortality of life and enjoyment of eternal good things in keeping your commandments. But when he had disobeyed you, the true God who created him, and had been led astray by the deceit of the serpent, and had been subjected to death by his own transgressions, you, O God, expelled him in your righteous judgment from paradise into this world, and turned him back to the earth from which he was taken, dispensing to him the salvation by rebirth which is in your Christ. For you did not turn away finally from your creature, O good one, nor forget the works of your hands, but you visited him in many ways through the bowels of your mercy. You sent forth prophets; you performed works of power through your saints who were pleasing to you in every generation; you spoke to us through the mouths of your servants [118] the prophets, foretelling to us the salvation that should come; you gave the Law for our help; you set angels as guards over us.

But when the fullness of time had come, you spoke to us in your Son himself, through whom also you made the ages, who, being the reflection of your glory and the impress of your substance, and bearing all things by the word of his power, thought it not robbery to be equal with you, the God and Father, but he who was God before the ages was seen on earth and lived among men; he was made flesh from a holy virgin and humbled himself, taking the form of a slave; he was conformed to the body of our humiliation that he might conform us to the image of his glory. For since through man sin had entered into the world, and through sin death, your only-begotten Son, who is in your bosom, O God and Father, being born of a woman, the Holy Mother of God and ever-Virgin Mary, born under the law, was pleased to condemn sin in his flesh, that those who died in Adam should be made alive in him, your Christ. And having become a citizen of this world, he gave us commandments of salvation, turned us away from the error of the idols, and brought us to the knowledge of you, the true God and Father; he gained us for himself, a peculiar people, a royal priesthood, a holy nation; and when he had cleansed us with water and sanctified us by the Holy Spirit, he gave himself as a ransom to death, by which we were held, having been sold under sin. By means of the cross he descended into hell, that he might fill all things with himself, and loosed the pains of death; he rose again on the third day, making a way to resurrection from the dead for all flesh, because it was not possible for the prince of life to be conquered by corruption, and became the first fruits of those who had fallen asleep, the first-born from the dead, so that he might be first in all ways among all things. And ascending into the heavens, he sat down at the right hand of the majesty in the highest, and will also come to reward each man according to his works. And he left us memorials of his saving passion, these things which we have set forth according to his commandments.

For when he was about to go out to his voluntary and laudable and life-giving death, in the night in which he gave himself up for the life of the world, he took bread in his holy and undefiled hands and showed it to you, the God and Father, gave thanks, blessed, sanctified, and broke it, and gave it to his holy disciples and apostles, saying, "Take, eat; this is my body, which is broken for you for the forgiveness of sins."

People: Amen.

Likewise also he took the cup of the fruit of the vine and mixed it, gave thanks, blessed, sanctified, and gave it to his holy disciples and apostles, saying, "Drink from this, all of you; this is my blood, which is shed for you and for many for the forgiveness of sins. <*People:* Amen.> Do this for my remembrance. For as often as you eat this bread and drink this cup, you proclaim my death, you confess my resurrection."

Therefore, Master, we also, remembering his saving Passion, his life-giving cross, his three-day burial, his resurrection from the dead, his ascension into heaven, his session at your right hand, God and Father, and his glorious and fearful second coming; (*aloud*) offer[-ing] you your own from your own, in all and through all,

People: we hymn you, <we bless you, we give you thanks, O Lord, and pray to you, our God.>

Therefore, Master all-holy, we also, your sinful and unworthy servants, who have been held worthy to minister at your holy altar, not for our righteousness, for we have done nothing good upon earth, but for your mercies and compassions which you have poured out richly upon us, with confidence approach your holy altar. And having set forth the likeness of the holy body and blood of your Christ, we pray and beseech you, O holy of holies, in the good pleasure of your bounty, that your [all-]Holy Spirit may come upon us and upon these gifts set forth, and bless them and sanctify and show (*he signs the holy gifts with the cross three times, saying:*) this bread the precious body of our Lord and God and Savior Jesus Christ. Amen. And this cup the precious blood of our Lord and God and Savior Jesus Christ, [Amen.] which is shed for the life of the world <and salvation>. Amen <*thrice*>.

Prayer:

Unite with one another all of us who partake of the one bread and the cup into fellowship with the one Holy Spirit; and make none of us to partake of the holy body and blood of your Christ for judgment or for condemnation, but that we may find mercy and grace with all the saints who have been well-pleasing to you from of old, forefathers, Fathers, patriarchs, prophets, apostles, preachers, evangelists, martyrs, confessors, teachers, and every righteous spirit perfected in faith; (*aloud*) especially our all-holy, immaculate highly blessed <glorious> Lady, Mother of God and ever-Virgin Mary; (*while the diptychs are read by the deacon, the priest says the prayer:*) Saint John the <prophet,> forerunner and Baptist, <the holy and honored apostles,> this saint *N.* whose memorial we are keeping, and all your saints: at their entreaties, visit us, O God.

And remember all those who have fallen asleep in hope of resurrection to eternal life, and grant them rest where the light of your countenance looks upon them.

Again we pray you, Lord, remember your holy, catholic, and apostolic Church from one end of the world to the other, and grant it the peace which you purchased by the precious blood of your Christ, and [e]stablish this holy house until the consummation of the age, and grant it peace.

Remember, Lord, those who presented these gifts, and those for whom, and through whom, and on account of whom they presented them.

Remember, Lord, those who bring forth fruit and do good work in your holy churches and remember the poor. Reward them with rich and heavenly gifts. Grant them heavenly things for earthy, eternal things for temporal, incorruptible things for corruptible.

[The intercessions continue]

[Concluding Doxology]

. . . and grant us with one mouth and one heart to glorify and hymn your all-honorable and magnificent name, the Father and the Son and the Holy Spirit, now <and always and to the ages of ages.>

People: Amen.[8]

In the absence of creeds within the eucharistic liturgy, therefore, it was the public profession of faith by means of the eucharistic prayer that continued to shape and form the church in its Orthodox trinitarian faith.[9] But while this was certainly true for the Christian East, it is harder to make this claim for eucharistic praying in the West since, at Rome, at least, the single eucharistic prayer known as the Roman Canon lacked any explicit reference to the Holy Spirit until the concluding doxology ("Through him [Christ], with him, in him, in the unity of the Holy Spirit, all honor and glory . . ."). Known already by Ambrose of Milan[10] in the late fourth century, this lack of an explicit pneumatology may well be a sign of the Roman Canon's antiquity reflecting a time *before* the late fourth century. But even in the West a concern for strict doctrinal orthodoxy and against improvised prayers also appears. The following from the Council of Hippo (393) makes this clear:

Let no one in the prayers name the Father in place of the Son, or the Son in place of the Father. At the altar, prayer should always

---

[8] Translation from PEER, 116–23.

[9] On the liturgy bearing and confessing the orthodox faith of the church, see Jaroslav Pelikan, *Credo: Historical and Theological Guide to Creeds and Confessions of Faith in the Christian Tradition* (New Haven, CT: Yale University Press, 2003), 166ff. and 405ff. See also Hans-Joachim Schulz, *The Byzantine Liturgy: Symbolic Structure and Faith Expression* (New York: Pueblo, 1986), 142–58.

[10] See PEER, 143–46.

---

be directed to the Father. And if anyone should copy prayers from elsewhere, he should not use them unless he has first conferred with the more instructed brethren about them.[11]

While Josef Jungmann[12] and others took this as further evidentiary proof of the so-called classic structure of Christian prayer (always *to* the Father, *through* the Son, and *in* the Holy Spirit) in the eucharistic prayer itself, it appears, alternatively, to be establishing a post-Nicene and post-Constantinopolitan orthodox norm for eucharistic praying rather than reflecting some norm already in existence. In other words, if in 393 CE—well before Ephesus and Chalcedon—eucharistic prayers are not being addressed to Christ even in the West, it would make no sense for a council to decree that they shouldn't be.

At the end of chapter 2 I referred to the fact that the approach of Joseph Jungmann is still important and needs to be taken seriously with regard to the perceived loss of the theology of Christ as High Priest and Mediator precisely in his humanity after the trinitarian and christological councils, especially in the West.[13] While such an approach is less of an issue in the Christian East, though even there the liturgical Christ becomes viewed increasingly as "Christ our *God*," what happens in the West is that in those places where Arianism and semi-Arianism continued to be most influential, notably in the Iberian Peninsula and in Gaul, increased liturgical prayer addressed to Christ as God and even to the Trinity itself will become characteristic emphases. These developments continue to influence the development of Christian worship in the West, where eventually even devotional feasts in honor of the Holy Trinity will develop and ultimately become part of the liturgical calendar. Similarly, in Spain, where it is quite likely that one single immersion had always taken place at baptism

---

[11] Text as cited in Geoffrey Wainwright, *Doxology: The Praise of God in Worship, Doctrine and Life* (New York: Oxford University Press, 1980), 254–55.

[12] See Josef Jungmann, *The Place of Christ in Liturgical Prayer* (Collegeville, MN: Liturgical Press, 1989), 169.

[13] See especially Josef Jungmann, "The Defeat of Teutonic Arianism and the Revolution in Religious Culture in the Early Middle Ages," in idem, *Pastoral Liturgy* (New York: Herder & Herder, 1962), 1–104. See also the summary provided by Catherine Mowry LaCugna, *God for Us: The Trinity and Christian Life* (San Francisco: HarperCollins, 1991), 123ff.

accompanied by the baptismal formula, that single immersion was now viewed as indicative of an anti-Arian position since it was interpreted as ritually reflecting the One God and Three Persons formula, an interpretation with which Gregory the Great concurs, according to various Spanish authors and councils.[14]

If Jungmann and his disciples overstated what they believed to be the classic patterns for prayer in the time before Nicea and Constantinople, and ruled out of consideration other liturgical elements as idiosyncratic departures from some presumed norm, there is no question but that Jungmann's analysis is still helpful for looking at the later patristic period and the early Middle Ages in the West. That is, as Christ was increasingly worshiped according to his divinity and equality with the Father and the Holy Spirit, his active liturgical mediation via his incarnation and humanity, although theoretically maintained, was lost sight of and his humanity became associated primarily with the historical events of his life on earth, especially with his nativity and his passion and death. Not only will this give rise to what might be called Western "Christmas" and "Good Friday" or "Passion" pieties, with the two chief Christian symbols being the crèche and the crucifix and with public and private devotion centered on each and by contemplation or imitation, but the need for human mediation will come to be expressed by Mary and the saints who, as mediators rather than as intercessors, now enter to fill the gap that the incarnation was supposed to fill in the first place.

While one might lament these developments, and Jungmann's approach certainly can be criticized today as incomplete, as biased against medieval developments, and for not taking into account more of what we now recognize as the important role played by "popular piety" associated with the saints even before the Council of Nicea, this development is clearly related to the ongoing interplay between worship and doctrine. That is, it is orthodox doctrine that comes to shape liturgy as much as praying shapes that believing in the first place. And what we are dealing with here is precisely the reality that the historic Christian liturgy came to embody Orthodox trinitarian

---

[14] On this, see Christian McConnell, *Baptism in Visigothic Spain* (PhD diss., University of Notre Dame, 2005), 217–19.

and christological doctrine and, hence, continues to form worshipers even today in that trinitarian and christological Orthodox faith.

No single period in the history of the church, of course, should ever be considered a "Golden Age." Nevertheless, the liturgical and doctrinal developments and conciliar decisions of the fourth and fifth centuries do play a formative role in what is to be considered Orthodox Christianity both in East and West. While we might indeed lament the liturgical losses for which this period of history was responsible (e.g., the loss of Christ's high priestly mediation in his humanity and the concomitant increase in the mediation of Mary and the saints, or the increasing loss of indigenous traditions of worship brought about by the dominance of others), the fact is that contemporary worshipers cannot pretend that something called "orthodoxy" did not develop or that they can uncritically incorporate "earlier" practices into their worship as though everything is up for grabs doctrinally and liturgically. Indeed, some of the diverse practices we encounter in liturgical history die out because they did not, in fact, meet the criteria of the developing orthodox doctrinal positions. The uncoordinated form of the doxology, as we have seen, "Glory *to* the Father, *through* the Son, *in* the Holy Spirit," for example, became, against Arianism and semi-Arianism, the orthodox form of "Glory *to* the Father, and *to* the Son, and *to* the Holy Spirit" for good trinitarian reasons, even if the loss of Christ's role as active mediator may have been downplayed in the process. Epiphany baptism itself may have been suspect and so challenged in the name of orthodoxy because of possible Adoptionist or Arian christological overtones, a reason also occasionally given for the establishment of the December 25 feast of Christmas as the feast of the Nicene *homoousios*. Do not postbaptismal rites that emphasize the gift of the Holy Spirit in baptism or explicit epicleses of the Holy Spirit in the anaphora develop, at least in part, because of doctrinal concerns for the Spirit's divinity in the context of the Council of Constantinople and its aftermath? Do not written and approved anaphoras come to express this concern for orthodoxy in a context in which the orthodoxy of extemporaneous prayer could no longer be assumed? Does not the catechumenate itself, as we know it from the great fourth- and fifth-century mystagogues, develop from some very real pastoral reasons as the church sought to incorporate converts with some integrity and authenticity in a changed sociopolitical-economic context? Does not the very shape of the Syro-Byzantine anaphora come to function as the doxological profession of orthodox trinitarian faith long before there was an actual creed recited in the eucharistic liturgy? And, for that matter, does not the fact that all the churches of the ancient world came to embrace the historic episcopacy as a "sign" of communion with each other and of orthodox continuity with the apostolic faith against Gnosticism and other challenges to the church's identity at least serve as challenge to the ordering of ministries in the church today, especially among those who have chosen to separate themselves from this historic office? In all of these cases, doctrine checks doxology just as much as praying assists in the shaping of believing. So it has been ever since. The practice of Christian worship forms the belief of the church (*ut legem credendi lex statuat lex supplicandi*). In turn, worship itself is formed further by that belief and, further still, continues to form people into believers and disciples of the crucified and risen Lord.

Contemporary developments in Christian worship today around the world but especially in the United States—e.g., the increasing phenomenon of megachurches, the Church Growth Movement, the development of "seeker services," and the increasing notion within and across ecclesial lines that the church's liturgy is but "one" of several options for "worship"—challenge the historic priority of sacramental worship. And what appears to be at stake in this, I would submit, is a particular theological understanding of who God is and how God is believed to act in the world and church, a theological understanding expressed within and by the historic Christian liturgies. That is, the classic sacramental-liturgical tradition claims that the trinitarian God acts primarily vis-à-vis creation and humanity through means, instruments, mediation, in ways that are described as both incarnational and sacramental. And, as such, grounded in and formed by what today might be called the ecumenical-liturgical-sacramental tradition, we can no more view that foundational understanding of how God is believed to act as one "option" among several than we can fly in the face of canon, creed, and confession without thereby denying our own identity and separating ourselves from the historic orthodox Christian faith. As Ruth Meyers has written of this sacramental worldview:

> The ordinary elements of water, bread, and wine allow us to encounter Christ in ways readily accessible to our senses. *We meet Christ not*

in some abstract spiritual way, but in these very tangible substances that
by their use in worship permeate the very core of our being. An expansive
use of these symbols helps us glimpse the infinite, incomprehensible,
overflowing love of God in Christ Jesus.[15]

The historic liturgies, then, remain central for the churches today
because they embody what classic Christianity believes about God
and about how God acts for us in creation and salvation. Closely
related to this, Geoffrey Wainwright has written that "Without the
heartbeat of the sacraments at its center, a church will lack confidence
about the gospel message and about its own ability to proclaim that
message in evangelism, to live it out in its own internal fellowship,
and to embody it in service to the needy."[16] And, elsewhere he writes
that "[a] deeper replunging into its own tradition will . . . be necessary if the church is to survive in recognizable form, particularly in
our western culture."[17] And the goal in all this, of course, is not simply
ecclesiastical survival but faithfulness, fidelity to the God who acts
and works for human salvation through sacraments, people, and
communities and to the sacramental worldview that continues to
define and characterize classic Christianity in spite of its manifold
denominational diversity. This goal is well summarized in the words
of Frank Senn, who writes in the conclusion of his *Christian Worship:*
Catholic and Evangelical:

> the church must provide what people lack in order to offer meaning
> for their lives: a narratable world—a worldview that provides coher-
> ent meaning and a way of enacting it. If the world has come apart in
> postmodern nihilism, the church must redo the world. It must provide
> an aimless present with a usable past and a hope-filled future. . . .
> And if we face in our society's religiosity a gnostic tendency to seek
> to escape from the threats of natural decay, temporal limitations, and

---

[15] R. Meyers, "Responses," in *Open Questions in Worship*, vol. 1: *What Are the*
Essentials of Christian Worship?, ed. Gordon Lathrop (Minneapolis: Augsburg
Fortress, 1994), 27; emphasis is original.

[16] Geoffrey Wainwright, "The Sacraments in Wesleyan Perspective," in idem,
Worship with One Accord: Where Liturgy and Ecumenism Embrace (New York: Oxford, 1998), 106.

[17] Geoffrey Wainwright, "Renewing Worship: The Recovery of Classical Patterns," in *Worship with One Accord*, 138.

> political responsibility, *this can be at least countered with attention to the sacramental life, the historic liturgy, and traditional ecclesiastical polity.*[18]

If history is not normative, it is at least informative, and as the first few centuries demonstrate liturgically and doctrinally, what we say, pray, and do or don't do in our liturgies does matter with regard to what we believe because words and actions matter. Hence, a community that celebrates and receives Christ's Body and Blood in the Eucharist every Sunday; attends to the rubrical options and varieties already present in the official liturgical book(s); prays the trinitarian and christologically shaped eucharistic prayer(s), according to any time-honored anaphoral patterns; faithfully proclaims the lectionary readings; and tenaciously keeps the feasts and seasons of the liturgical year week after week, year after year, will be a different sort of community than one that is continually experimenting with "worship alternatives" and searching for something "better" to meet the so-called needs of worshipers and potential seekers alike. And I dare say that the first type of community will, undoubtedly, be more "orthodox" in its doctrinal-theological outlook because the liturgy it celebrates is formed by the orthodox-liturgical-doctrinal tradition. Why is this important? Because the liturgy is, first and foremost, the *opus Dei*, God's work for us, God's self-giving in trinitarian love, and so its primary purpose is not to permeate our lives with ritual but to permeate them with Christ by means of the Holy Spirit working through Word and Sacrament for the very building up of his Body, the church, and for the salvation and life of the world.[19] But, as we saw in the previous chapter, even this calls for verification or authentication in the "liturgy of the neighbor," in what the Christian East calls "the liturgy after the liturgy." *Ite, missa est!* "Go," the conclusion of the liturgy says to us, "you are sent on mission in the world." For *missa* (Mass) leads to *missio* (mission) and that mission, as we have seen, is primarily expressed in our work, which is, in the words of Nathan

---

[18] Frank C. Senn, *Christian Liturgy: Catholic and Evangelical* (Minneapolis: Fortress Press, 1997), 698; emphasis added.

[19] See Robert Taft, "What Does Liturgy Do? Toward a Soteriology of Liturgical Celebration: Some Theses," in idem, *Beyond East and West: Problems in Liturgical Understanding*, 2nd rev. and enlarged ed. (Rome: Pontifical Oriental Institute, 1997), 239–58.

Mitchell, for and to "a God who, in the cross of Jesus and in the bodies of the 'poor, the hungry, the thirsty, the naked, the imprisoned,' has become everything we believe a God is *not*."

Index